ADVENTURE
INWARD

A RISK TAKER'S
BOOK OF QUOTES

Compiled and Edited by

JONATHAN WUNROW

Life is Twisted Press

Cover design by Jonathan Wunrow and Bri Bruce
Cover Image courtesy Shutterstock
Photos by Jonathan Wunrow
Edited by Bri Bruce

Published by Life is Twisted Press, Kasaan, Alaska

Visit www.jonathanwunrow.com for more information.

PRAISE FOR *Adventure Inward*

Wunrow discusses why some take extreme risks, how it impacts on their lives and the lives of their loved ones, and how taking risks can make one feel truly alive. . . . it won't matter if you've never even been near a mountain or risked edging the speedometer of your car a mile or two over the speed limit. There are quotes in here that will speak directly to you. . . . [This book is] an inspirational call to live life fully. Settle in for a read, and listen to the voices collected in Adventure Inward: A Risk Taker's Book of Quotes. *They have a lot to say and it's all well worth hearing.*

- Jack Magnus, Readers' Favorite

Adventure Inward *consists of inspirational and humorous quotes designed to get readers thinking about their own course in life, and it reaches its own summit in tacking the bigger questions of life purpose. Even if you're not a natural risk-taker, it will provoke reflections on life's meaning that ultimately lead to transitions and changes. . . . And lest you think you need to be a sports enthusiast to properly absorb his adages, let it be said that the only prerequisite is an interest in self-growth and understanding life paths and transition points. If it's an inspirational and thought-provoking reader that's desired, packed with quotes and insights for personal advancement, then* Adventure Inward *more than fits the bill.*

- D. Donovan, eBook Reviewer, Midwest Book Review

A wonderful book. Adventure Inward *does a great job of explaining many existential issues concerning life, death, and one's purpose. I would definitely recommend this book to readers who like extreme sports and also to anyone interesting in contemplating life's mysteries.*

- Avery Griffin, Author of *The Demon Rolmar*

An excellent compilation of inspiring, humorous, and thought-provoking quotes sure to get anyone, no matter their hobbies, pastimes, or interests, thinking deeply about their world and what it means for us as humans to look inside ourselves. Each chapter is adorned with Wunrow's clear voice and unfailing insight into the human psyche in the presence of "risk" and the many ways this can be interpreted. . . . Wunrow has done a wonderful job writing and compiling this book. It will make an impression and spur you to thought.

- Bri Bruce, Surfer and Author of *The Weight of Snow*

I loved this book. It is surprisingly relevant to anyone's life. A good quote can inspire, transcend, counter negative thoughts, help us dream, allow us to escape, validate our thinking and beliefs, and offer basic truths. The quotes, proverbs, and sayings Jonathan Wunrow has collected from people of all kinds during his years of mountain climbing experience can translate to life itself.

- Amanda Mac, Something to Ponder About Book Reviews

Inspiring reading! Wunrow has written a wonderful gem for all those who appreciate, or want to better understand, the human urge to adventure. The author presents his own personal insights in uniquely themed chapters that are jam-packed with thought-provoking and funny quotations.

- Logan, Amazon Customer Review

This book is dedicated to the dreamers, to the risk takers, and to the misfits.

TABLE OF CONTENTS

Climbing is a metaphor for life itself. There is the aspiration and the uncertainty, the journey and the risk, the success and its concomitant satisfaction. Life on the mountain becomes a simplified model of life in the harried world, a model with equal anguish, but one whose challenges are carved into perfect definition. We win here, and we know we can win elsewhere.

- Don Mellor

ADVENTURE
INWARD

A RISK TAKER'S
BOOK OF QUOTES

INTRODUCTION

Since the first time that I tied onto the end of a rope at age fourteen, mountain climbing and adventuring have been part of my life. I've never been a world-class mountaineer or climber, and I have only met a couple of them in my lifetime,[1] but I've always sought out adventure, and I've tried to be open to allowing adventure to seek me out as well. We all know the story of Helen Keller, for whom every aspect of daily life had to be an adventure. With no sense of sight or sound to navigate from moment to moment, it's no wonder that she is quoted as saying,

---

I once spent a brief evening in 1984 with Jeff Lowe and John Roskelley, sharing a beer in a small guesthouse in Namche Bazaar in the Solu Khumbu Region of Mount Everest, Nepal. Roskelley and Lowe had just completed a dramatic alpine ascent of Tawoche's northwest face. The climb is documented in Roskelley's book *Last Days*

1

"Life is either a daring adventure, or nothing." For most of the rest of us, seeing life as a daring adventure is a matter of perception, and a matter of choice. Making the choice to view one's life as a series of endless adventures, and risks that are waiting to be taken, can make every day, and virtually every moment, something to be excited about and to look forward to.

Given the choice, adventure sounds a lot more interesting to me, than doing nothing. I've learned over the years that when our eyes and spirit are wide open to what is possible, daring adventures come our way in all sorts of forms, not just through the extreme adventures of surfing and climbing, hang gliding and mountain biking, snow boarding and heli-skiing, but also through the daily activities of parenting, finding ways to help other people, going to work, creating and maintaining relationships, living day-to-day, and playing a meaningful role in the world around us. So, as the Don Mellor quote at the start of this book reminds us, adventuring and taking risks are metaphors for life itself.

Although big wall climber Chuck Pratt was right when he said, "writing about climbing is boring," and that he "would rather go climbing," there are lots of connections between extreme sports and good writing, especially between extreme sports and good quotes. The reason I felt compelled to write *Adventure Inward: A Risk Taker's Book of Quotes* is because quotes help me understand concepts and feelings that I have a hard time putting into words. Most other people have a difficult time understanding the things we do and the decisions we make as risk takers and extreme sports enthusiasts. The risks we take usually aren't based on "common sense" or easily identified rewards. Over the years, I've found that quotes spoken or written by other risk takers have helped me feel less alone. Extreme sports enthusiasts have more depth than we often get credit for, and this book is for risk takers who want to spend some time pondering why we do what we do.

I've always been a seeker of quotes, or more often than not they seem to find me, usually at times when I need to make sense out of what's going on around me. Just as essayist Joseph Epstein declared, "I'm seeking clues to explain life's oddities," I have sought quotes to provide me with clues about life.

A good quote at the right time can:

- Inspire

- Transcend

- Counter negative thoughts

- Help us dream

- Instruct

- Allow us the opportunity to escape the moment

- Validate our thinking and beliefs

- Offer basic truths

Quotes can also help us not feel so alone. The knowledge that someone else, in some past time, felt the same way I am feeling in this moment brings a sense of connectedness and normalcy. This need to feel connected to others through common words and thoughts are what C.S. Lewis was referring to when he wrote, "We read to know we're not alone." Over the years, I've found only a few people who seem to understand why I keep heading back into the mountains to climb. Having so few risk-taking peers can be lonely sometimes, so when I discover a good quote that speaks to me, I know that I'm not alone.

I have found that after gathering quotes for the past forty years, and after engaging in countless adventures over those same forty years, quotes not only inform my life in general, helping me be a better person, but they help me be a better climber. Just discovering a good quote means little if it doesn't move us to act. The wisdom of others can move us to rethink, to change, to do. Khalil Gibran wrote, "Sayings remain meaningless until they are embodied in habits," which, to me, is a much more elegant way of saying, "Talk is cheap."

I used to think that climbing to the top of a high peak like Denali in Alaska or Sajama in Bolivia was an end in itself. The goal was to summit, and success and failure was determined by whether or not I got to the top. For other risk takers, the goal is to brave a Class V rapid, or BASE jump off the Perrine Bridge above the Snake River, or surf a great wave in Australia, or mountain bike an expert Grade 5, or to heli-ski outside of Cordova, Alaska. To be completely honest, I still think this way most days, but I've also learned that climbing is a metaphor for the things that I do when I'm not climbing. The same can be said for any extreme sport or adventure. Risk taking is a metaphor for the joys and challenges and boredom and wonder of everyday life. What I learn on the mountain helps me make sense of what's going on around me and inside of me when I'm not on the mountain. Over the years, quotes have helped me capture that essence of what I am learning. Nineteenth century author Charles E. Montague understood the metaphor for life that risk taking represents when he wrote, "To climb up rocks is like all the rest of your life, only simpler and safer." Does that ring true for you, too?

I have been collecting quotes since I was in junior high school. My "quote file" has grown over the years from a few inspirational clippings in church bulletins and magazines, to a half-dozen files thickly crammed with thousands upon thousands of quotes. When I read something in a book that resonates with me, I copy it onto a scrap of paper. When I hear a line in a movie that I think is cool, I write it on whatever is within reach. When a friend or a total stranger says something that strikes a chord, I try to memorize it until I have a second to jot it down. Over the years, my collection of other people's musings and reflections has grown.

In going through all of the quotes that I have gathered, I realized how truly personal and individualized quotes are. What inspires me may not inspire you, and what inspired me yesterday may not make any sense to me at all today. Many of the quotes that I gathered when I was younger just don't speak to me any more and now I wonder why I had ever saved them. I know that at one point or another in my life, the quote that I clipped or jotted down inspired me, and this inspiration gives me hope. Inspiration helps me get through long days of office boredom spent between one adventure and the next. It allows me to understand a traumatic or confusing event, and provides the motivation and determination I need to sustain the long slogs up the King's Trench on Mount Logan or through the endless jungles of Suriname or Belize in search of country high points.

There are lots of famous people, as well as not so famous people, who have said interesting things that risk takers and adventurers can relate to. Every once in a while an extreme sports enthusiasts comes up with something insightful and wise about how their sport and risk taking informs and enriches the rest of life.

Adventure Inward: A Risk Taker's Book of Quotes contains quotes from adventurers and non-adventurers alike. I have also included a lot of Buddhist quotes in this book. Many climbers and adventurers have recognized a connection between Buddhist teachings and what we learn from the risks we take and during long silent hours of introspection, brushes with death, and feelings of connection to all things. World-class climber Jonathan Waterman noted in his book *The Quotable Climber* that there are a myriad of climbers who, if not practicing Buddhists, embrace the ideals of Buddhism. The same can be said for extreme sport enthusiasts, regardless of their sport of choice.

Speaking of Jonathan Waterman, about the time that I was nearing completion of this book, I ran across a copy of Jonathan Waterman's book, *The Quotable Climber*, published in 2002. I immediately felt disappointed in realizing that someone (and a famous climber at that) had already written the book that I had been thinking about writing for years. As I read Waterman's book of climber's quotes, I realized that we were coming at the topic of relating quotes and climbing from two very different perspectives. Waterman's *The Quotable Climber* is subtitled, "Literary, Humorous, Inspirational, and Fearful Moments in Climbing." Waterman describes his book as a collection of "pithy sayings" and "obscure and uncensored witticisms" about the sport of mountaineering, mostly from mountaineers.

My approach to *Adventure Inward* has been to create a collection of quotes, gathered from all kinds of people and persuasions that can help climbers, adventurers, and all sorts of other people gain a perspective about life, death, purpose, and meaning. *Adventure Inward* offers a large selection of quotes for a much wider audience.

So, how should you use this book? My suggestion is to keep it on your bed stand, or at the office on your desk, in the top flap of your backpack or dry bag, within arm's reach of your toilet, on the dashboard of your car, or on top of the TV. Put it someplace visible. Don't hide it on your bookshelf next to all of your other adventure books. Keep it in a place where you will see it every day. Take a few moments and open it when you are bored, frustrated, sad, unmotivated, or unsure, or when you are getting psyched about a new adventure, feeling content, or laying in your sleeping bag in the rarified air of a high mountain. Randomly choose a page and start reading. Read just long enough to find one or two quotes that connect to where your head is at that very moment, close the book, and know that you're not alone.

When you read or hear a good quote, whether from this book or elsewhere, write it down, tape it to your computer screen, fold the slip of paper in half and put it in your wallet, stick it to the mirror in your bathroom so you see it every morning when you wake up, tape it to your helmet, thumb tack them all over your office wall, read them to start your day, read them when you need to feel inspired, send one to a friend, text one to your son, email one to your lover, or save it for the next time you really need it.

WHY PLAY A RISKY GAME?

Extreme adventurers (and their loved ones) have been pondering this question forever. Part of the reason that the answer is so elusive is that our motives aren't the kinds of things that society in general chooses to reward. For the vast majority of us, risk taking does not bring financial reward or public recognition. Often those closest to us don't understand why we do it and feign interest when we talk about it. My guess is that the average life expectancy of extreme sports enthusiasts is shorter than that of others. Their bodies wear out quicker as well. Even most risk takers themselves can't quite put their finger on why they continue to do what they do. The reasons are varied, and can often change. The reasons may be as different and as unique as the DNA of each of us.

The same question can be asked about any endeavor in life, any passion, any vocation, or any pastime. Why do we do it? Why did we choose it over other options? Why, in

9

the face of hardship and risk or boredom and insecurity, do we continue on the path we've chosen? Or why do we choose to abandon a path that seemed right for so long?

My dad used to say to me, "You climb because it 'hurts so good.'" He thought I must like the pain and suffering that often accompanies a challenging adventure. Why else, he'd wonder aloud, would I do it? My oldest brother has often said that I climb because I don't know how to relax. He has observed that even on a "vacation" I have to keep moving and find something hard or challenging to do. My wife has stopped trying to figure out why I climb. She just accepts it. Then again, she runs marathons and for the life of me I can't figure that one out.

There are many motivations that fuel risk takers and adventurers and the choices they make. The answers to why we choose to do what we do are sometimes funny and nonsensical, and sometimes deep and meaningful. Occasionally, the answers are spiritual and eternal, and almost always they are very personal. Even the most famous adventurers don't seem to be quite sure why they persist. Maybe some of us take risks just for something to do, or as Sir Edmund Hillary once wrote, "you climb for the hell of it."

So if you are struggling with trying to understand why you do what you do, whether it's canyoneering, snowboarding, surfing, scuba diving, or free-ride mountain biking, see if any of these quotes resonate with you. Feel free to substitute your sport or passion when you see the word "climbing," and see whether the statements connect with your soul.

What you do on your own scale for your own soul is all that matters. I don't have to do things that other people consider as difficult anymore. To climb a mountain to see if I can keep from falling off is no reason. To climb a mountain to celebrate my limbs, the sky, my friends, seems better . . . I wish to fulfill myself in dance not words. Walking skillfully along the top of the world we may receive a priceless vista of our lives and see that which is truly important to us. We may never be able to make sense of why this is so, and if our discoveries are great they always seem to defy words.

- Jeff Salz

What we get from this adventure is just sheer joy. And joy is, after all, the end of life. We do not live to eat and make money. We eat and make money to be able to enjoy life. That is what life means, and what life is for.

- George Leigh Mallory

The more you live, the less you die.

- Janice Joplin

What's the difference between a fairy tale and a mountain story? A fairy tale begins, "Once upon a time . . . " and a mountain story begins, "No Shit! There I was . . . "

- River Guide Julie

11

Freedom is a need. I have a cat. People feed this cat; they pet this cat; they give the cat everything he needs. But every time the window is open just a little, he runs away.

- Dalai Lama

A climber's day always starts at the crux; getting out of bed.

- Unknown

I love climbing because it feels so good when I stop.

- Karl Baba

I didn't actually want coffee, but I poured myself a cup, just because the pot was there. I guess I'm a lot like George Mallory, who had similar motivation for climbing Mount Everest.

- Chuck Bonner

For if you can't understand that there is something in a man which responds to the challenge of this mountain and goes out to meet it, that the struggle is the struggle of life itself, upward and forever upward, then you won't see why we go.

- George Leigh Mallory

Because I'm grumpy when I'm not climbing.

- Doug Scott

Because we're insane.

> \- Warren Harding

If you don't scale the mountain, you can't view the plane.

> \- Chinese Proverb

Climbing is not a battle with the elements, nor against the law of gravity. It's a battle against oneself.

> \- Walter Bonatti

The first question which you will ask and which I must answer is this, "What is the use of climbing Mount Everest?" And my answer must at once be, "It is of no use." We shall not bring back a single bit of gold or silver, not a gem, nor any coal or iron. We shall not find a single foot of earth that can be planted with crops to raise food. It's no use. So, if you cannot understand that there is something in man which responds to the challenge of this mountain and goes out to meet it, that the struggle is the struggle of life itself upward and forever upward, then you won't see why we go.

> \- George Leigh Mallory

First there is a mountain,
Then there is no mountain,
Then there is.

> \- Lyrics of "There is a Mountain" by Donovan Leitch

Without gravity we wouldn't have a sport.

- Matthew Ketterling

Maybe Himalayan climbing is just a bad habit, like smoking, of which one says with cavalier abandon, "Must give this up some day before it kills me."

- Greg Child

I have been constantly asked, with a covert sneer, "Did it repay you?"—A question which involves the assumption that one wants to be repaid, as though the labor were not itself part of the pleasure.

- Sir Leslie Stephen

We like to look sixteen and bored shitless.

- David Johanson of the band New York Dolls

How is the world a better place if we climbed it (Corcovado) or didn't? . . . If it's important that we climbed it, made a second ascent and wrote it up for history books, then it's a failure. But if it's just that we were out for a good adventure, then we were successful.

- Yvon Chouinard

It's as close as we can come to flying.

- Margaret Young

A man does not climb a mountain without bringing some of it away with him and leaving something of himself upon it.

- Sir Martin Conway

We have to understand that the world can only be grasped by action, not by contemplation.

- Jacob Bronowski

You lose it if you talk about it.

- Ernest Hemingway

We never grow tired of each other,
the mountain and I.

- Li Po

To venture causes anxiety, but not to venture is to lose one's self . . . And to venture in the highest is precisely to become conscious of one's self.

- Søren Kierkegaard

*And this is what really counts—not just achieving things . . .
but the advantage you have taken of your opportunities and
the opportunities you created. Each of us has to discover
his own path—of that I am sure. Some paths will be
spectacular and others peaceful and quiet—and who is to
say which is the most important? For me the most
rewarding moments have not always been the great
moments—for what can surpass a tear on your departure,
joy on your return, or a trusting hand in yours? Most of all I
am thankful for the tasks still left to do—for the adventures
still lying ahead . . . Yes, there is plenty left to do.*

- Sir Edmund Hillary

This is the fucking life! No?

- Jean Afanassieff, member of the first
French team to Summit Mt. Everest)

*What are we then, those of us who like to dangle in the
void and test the cutting edge of our ability?*

- Apsley Cherry-Garrard

No pay, no prospects, not much pleasure.

- H.W. Tilman, from an ad in the *London Times*
encouraging climbers to join him on an expedition

Man overcomes himself, affirms himself, and realizes himself in the struggle towards the summit, toward the absolute.

- L. Davies

Naked of life, naked of warmth and safety, bare to the sun and stars, beautiful in its stark loneliness, the mountain waits.

- Elizabeth Knowlton

Probing the edges of what may be possible is the only thing I know how to do. It is too late now at my age to stop, not to do it. And more than anything—I am like a child—I would always be unhappy if I didn't try.

- Reinhold Mesner

I suppose the first sight of a mountain is always the best. Later, when you are waiting to start, you may grow to hate the brute, because you are afraid. And when, finally, you are climbing, you are never aware of the mountain as a mountain: it is merely so many little areas of rock to be worked out, in tens of handholds, and footholds and effort, like so many chess problems. But when you first see it in the distance, remote and beautiful and unknown, then there seems some reason for climbing. That, perhaps, is what Mallory meant by his comment, "Because it's there."

- A. Alvarez

Always roaming with a hungry heart. I am a part of all that I have met, yet all experience is an arch where through gleams that untraveled world whose margin fades forever and forever, where I move . . . How dull it is to pause.

- *Ulysses*

I not only look for adventure, but adventure looks for me, and it finds me often.

- Frank Buckles, the oldest living World War I veteran who died at the age of 110

The struggle itself towards the heights is enough to fill a man's heart.

- Albert Camus

If I made my choices based on a need to avoid fear of the unknown, then I wouldn't be here.

- Jon Wunrow, while climbing Mount Logan

Contemplation within activity is a million times better than contemplation within stillness.

- Hakuin

Even the descent was fraught with sucking.

- Unknown Climber

I'm glad I did it, partly because it was well worth it, and chiefly because I shall never have to do it again.

- Mark Twain

We're on top of this fucker.

- Kim Momb, from Mt. Everest's summit

Somewhere between the base and the summit is the answer to why we climb.

- Unknown Climber

Mountains should be climbed with as little effort as possible and without desire. The reality of your own nature should determine the speed. If you become restless, speed up. If you become winded, slow down. You climb the mountain in an equilibrium between restlessness and exhaustion. Then, when you're no longer thinking ahead, each footstep isn't just a means to an end but a unique event in itself. This leaf has a jagged edge. This rock looks loose. From this place the snow is less visible, even though closer. These are things you should notice anyway. To live only for some future goal is shallow. It's the side of the mountains which sustain life, not the top.

- Excerpt from *Zen and the Art of Motorcycle Maintenance* by Rober Pirsig

I would rather be poor with lots of stories to tell, than rich with nothing to say.

- Kari Lundgren

Climbing would be a great, truly wonderful thing if it weren't for all the damn climbing.

- John Ohrenschall

Clouds too know the flavor of this mountain life.

- Ching An

When you get there, there isn't any there there.

- Gertrude Stein

I seek potential value in the nothingness of my pursuit.

- Unknown

Climbing is a means of self-expression.

- L. Davies

In action, anxiety disappears.

- Unknown

Climbing is an addiction. We are far worse off than any drug addict could ever imagine. Our curse takes us to physical and mental highs and satisfies some urge to challenge ourselves. We feel healthy and happy and we don't see that it could ever be wrong to do what we do.

- Linda Givler, two years after her husband's climbing death in Alaska

When you have the energy and the drive, and you don't try to live life to the fullest, then what are you doing?

- Jack Tackle describing Alex Lowe

I learn by going where I have to go.

- Theodore Roethke

Maybe climbing is just a "place to go"?

- Jon Wunrow

In justification, I would argue (and still do) that it is in the mountains that I have pursued dreams, grown confident, learned to survive, acquired a love of the wilderness, and shared special moments with kindred spirits. My bond with high places has defined my professional and person life. Mountains are my spiritual home; more than any thing else, they have shaped who I am and how I relate to the world and those who share it with me.

- Tom Hornbein

*In the misty blue haze, jagged peaks appear as if joined.
When will I climb and set foot there, to gaze on all the
world below?*

- Chia Tao

The old man must have stopped our car two dozen
times to climb out and gather into his hands the small
toads, blinded by our lights and leaping into the road, like
drops of rain.

The rain was falling, a mist about his white hair, and I
kept saying, "You can't save them all. Accept it. Get back
in. We've got places to go." But, leathery hands full of wet
brown life, knee deep in summer roadside grass, he just
smiled and said, "They have places to go, too."

-Joseph Bruchac

*It is in your act that you exist, not in your body. Your act is
yourself, and there is no other you.*

- Antoine de Saint-Exupery

Climbing might be hard, but it's easier than growing up.

- Ed Sklar

Talk does not cook rice.

- Chinese Proverb

Few among men are they who cross over to the further shore. The others merely run up and down the bank on the side.

- Dhammapada

From a certain point onward there is no turning back. This is the point that must be reached.

- Franz Kafka

I follow my impulsive feet wherever they might go.
My body is a pine tree surrounded by the snow.
Sometimes I simply stand beside a flowing stream.
Sometimes I chase a drifting cloud past another peak.

- Han-shan TeCh'ing

We must, in all activities, push to do more difficult and challenging things. But not to beat our fellows, rather to find ourselves.

- Charles S. Houston

We passed a lifetime untangling the line. And came to our senses with the cows in the dell.

- Rene Daumal

Is it the summit, crowing the day? How cool and quiet!
We're not exultant; but delighted, joyful; soberly astonished
. . . Have we vanquished an enemy? None but ourselves.
Have we gained success? That word means nothing here.

- George Leigh Mallory

In the light of flowers
I travel
Just for the sake of traveling.

- Soen Nakagawa

I find that rock climbing is the finest, healthiest sport in the
whole world. It is much healthier than most; look at
baseball, where 10,000 sit on their ass to watch a handful of
players.

- John Salathé

Truth is given, not to be contemplated, but to be done. Life
is an action, not a thought.

- F.W. Robertson

The path up and down is one and the same.

- Heraclitus

If you want to climb it badly enough, you will. So . . . why bother?

- Doug Scott

I have not conquered Everest, it has merely tolerated me.

- Peter Habeler

The mountains reserve their choice gifts for those who stand upon their summits.

- Francis Younghusband

Ever since a small boy, I have loved just to look at the mountains, to see them in different lights and from different angles, to feel their rough rock under my fingers and the breath of their winds against my feet . . . I am in love with the mountains.

- Wilfred Noyce

Our poignant adventure, our self-sought perils on a line of unreason to the summit of a superfluous rock, have no rational or moral justification.

- Geoffrey Winthrop Young

There are only three sports—mountain climbing, bull fighting, and motor racing—all the rest being game.

- Ernest Hemmingway

Why? Why, why, why do I do this?

- Chuck Pratt

The climbing as a whole is not very esthetic or enjoyable; it is merely difficult.

- Yvon Chouinard

If it is a shame to be the second man on Mount Everest, then I will have to live with this shame.

- Tenzing Norgay

Anyone who says that they are having fun up here is flat out lying!

- Russ Walling

For a time I play catch while the children sing;
Then it is my turn.
Playing like this, time slips away.
Passersby point and laugh, asking,
"What is the reason for such foolishness?"
I only bow.
Even if I answered, they would not understand.
Look around! There is nothing else but this.

- Ryokan

Q: Why do mountain climbers rope themselves together?
A: To prevent the sensible ones from going home!

- Unknown Climber

Near the foot of the mountain we visited a yogi who dwelled in a hollow tunneled beneath a boulder. He pondered our notion of climbing Shivling and said, "First travel, then struggle, finally calm."

- Greg Child

Life is brought down to the basics: if you are warm, regular, healthy, not thirsty or hungry, then you are not on a mountain.

- Chris Darwin

We learn something by doing it. There is no other way.

- John Holt

The distinguishing mark of true adventures, is that it is often no fun at all while they are actually happening.

- Kim Stanley Robinson

Each fresh peak ascended teaches something.

- Sir Martin Conway

*It is not the goal of grand alpinism to face peril, but it is one
of the tests one must undergo to deserve the joy of rising
for an instant above the state of crawling grubs.*

- Lionel Terray

*From early days, I found that climbing is the only thing in
life that gave more than momentary satisfaction.*

- Dougal Haston

*Climbing at altitude is like hitting your head against a brick
wall—it's great when you stop.*

- Chris Darwin

*I went to the mountain seeking enlightenment.
There was no enlightenment on the mountain.*

- Soen Nakagawa

It's not the mountains we conquer, but ourselves.

- Sir Edmund Hillary

*The ancient Greeks asked oracles for answers; Native
Americans fasted in the desert;
I go climbing.*

- Steph Davis

QUALITIES OF AN EXTREME ADVENTURER

There are a myriad of answers to the question "What qualities, both internal and external, are necessary to be good at what one does?" The question takes an added twist when we ask, "What qualities make a good or successful risk taker, or a good adventurer?" An even more important question is how do we define "good" and who gets to do the defining? There are days when I think that the best climbers are the ones who are in the best physical shape, have the biggest muscles, can maintain a high oxygen saturation level in their blood, and can carry the heaviest loads at altitude. I usually think this way when I'm gasping for air, with an overloaded backpack, and my spindly legs are about to give out. I'm sure you have similar adjectives and phrases that define the best at your sport.

Other days I firmly believe that the best risk takers are the fearless ones: the solo free climbers who are scaling grade 5.13 climbs, hundreds of feet above the ground with no ropes or anchors, or those that take on the big vicious mountains like K2 and Annapurna where the survival rates and summit rates are about equal. Being able to face and manage fear and the unknown is an important strength when taking on extreme sports like big wave surfing, BASE jumping, or skydiving.

Commitment, determination, and patience are key to dealing with the day-in and day-out mental, emotional, and physical grind of training and participating in extreme sports. They are also important characteristics needed in order for one to keep coming back, maybe one hundred times, to work out the moves of a difficult boulder problem or the challenge of an out-of-bounds run while skiing.

Are wisdom, intelligence, and problem solving skills crucial to what makes a successful adventurer? Maybe its knowing when to accept defeat, acknowledging when the wave isn't worth the risk, or the run is just too avalanche-prone today, understanding when it's time to pack up and go home despite the months of planning and large amounts of money that have been invested in an expedition. Maybe the "best" risk takers are the ones who are still alive to tell their tales. Or are the best the ones who died pushing beyond their limit while doing what they loved?

The same questions can be asked of any profession or pastime or passion. What makes a good teacher? What makes a good lover? What makes a good human being? What makes a good father or mother? These are all questions that we need to ask and to answer for ourselves. The answers to what makes a good adventurer or a good human being are personal, and sometimes they aren't very clear. Over the centuries, many people have offered their wisdom so that you can come to your own conclusions.

The best climber in the world is the one who is having the most fun.

- Alex Lowe

If you want to be a good polar traveler, get a man without too much muscle, with good physical tone, and let his mind be on wires of steel.

- Apsley Cherry-Garrard

Commit so something. Put your balls on the line. And then figure it out.

- Joel Runyon

The best training was to go to the pub, drink five quarts of beer, and talk about climbing.

- Ron Fawcett

Endurance produces character, and character produces hope.

- Unknown

Continuous effort—not strength or intelligence—is the key to unlocking our potential.

- Winston Churchill

Technique and ability alone do not get you to the top—it is the willpower that is the most important. This willpower you cannot buy with money or be given by others—it rises from your heart.

- Junko Tabei, the first woman
to climb Mt. Everest

For one thing, we were both rather lazy . . . an important quality of the serious climber.

- Warren Harding

Climbing is a not a battle with the elements, nor against the law of gravity. It's a battle against oneself.

- Walter Bonatti

The way of the sage is to act but not to compete.

- Lao-Tzu

The only way to be cool is accidentally.

- Ben Taylor

You see the ball, you hit the ball.
They hit the ball, you catch the ball.
You catch the ball, you throw the ball.
That's it.

- Kirby Puckett

You don't see farmers as climbers. You see city people. Farmers don't need to climb.

- Yvon Chouinard

The wanderer: let that be my name.

- Basho

Any human being, however meek and unambitious they may think themselves, can develop a mixture of single-minded desire to fulfill a particular goal. The quantum leap is the moment of investigation, that first push to make the stone roll. Thereafter all manner of undreamed-of outside factors will fall into place. Once the stone is rolling and the die is cast, most people will find they can keep going against the odds.

- Ranulph Fiennes

Height has nothing to do with it, it is your strength that counts.

- Lynn Hill

He did each single thing as if he did nothing else.

- Charles Dickens

I don't have any friends, and my nuts are too small.

- Anonymous rock climber on a bad day

Until one is committed there is hesitancy, the chance to draw back, always in effect. Concerning all acts of initiative there is one elementary truth, the ignorance of which kills splendid plans. . . . That the moment one definitely commits oneself, then providence moves too. All sorts of things happen to help what would otherwise have never occurred.

- William Murray

Rules alone are rules, and will continue to be broken by those kids in desperate need of attention.

- Leslie Skooglund

I have always thought that heroism must be rarer at dawn than in the evening—I often observed the fact in alpine huts: in the evening everyone is praying for fine weather the next day, and when the next day comes they wish that it was raining.

- Ren Dittert

Humility is the key to being a good alpinist.

- Barry Blanchard

I wouldn't go there if I were you. They steal from the store and they smell and they wear rags and even piss right outside their tents. I tell you, it's like a leper colony, that place.

- Yosemite Lodge bellman trying to dissuade
a girl from visiting Camp 4 in 1962

As a kid I knew two things to be self-evident. Flying: believe it and it'll happen. Superpowers: bound to be something— spinach or whatever will do the trick. Climbing is my flying, and coffee is my spinach.

- Peter Croft

The less effort, the faster and more powerful you will be.

- Bruce Lee

For we are a nation of shopkeepers. And so you will sledge nearly alone, but those with whom you sledge will not be shopkeepers.

- Apsley Cherry-Garrard

Trust only movement. Life happens at the level of events not of words. Trust movement.

- Alfred Adler

So a try mind is more important than any Zen master. If you say, "I can," then you can do something. If you say "I cannot," then you cannot do anything. Which do you like?

- Seung Sahn

As far as I'm concerned, if someone eliminates the mental part of climbing, then we might as well all be playing miniature golf.

- Greg Opland

In fact, I think you should add your body fat to the rating of a climb, to get a true measure of your inner climber. So climbing a 5.7 with 22 percent body fat is way harder than climbing a 5.14 with 3 percent body fat.

- Mike Yukish

There are two kinds of climbers: those who climb because their heart sings when they're in the mountains, and all the rest.

- Alex Lowe

Don't complain. Accept things as they are and satisfy yourself with what you have, right now. You should think, "This is the only reality I can see, I can have, I can experience."

- Shunryu Suzuki

In all the splendor of solitude . . . it is a test of myself, and one thing I loathe is to have to test myself in front of other people.

- Naomi Uemura

Anyone need advice on making the transition from 5.12 to 5.11?

- Andy Cairns

The climb waits for someone with stainless steel testicles.

- Roger Briggs

If you don't take care of yourself, the best equipment in the world can't prevent frostbite.

- Jonathan Waterman

Climbers are masters of denial.

- Wanda Rutkiewicz

Consciousness is in the first place not a matter of "I think," but of "I can."

- Maurice Merleau-Ponty

Rock climbers know that it is usually easier to climb up a steep rock face, than to down-climb. As you look up, carefully and thoughtfully, from the bottom at the seemingly impossible climb above, you can eventually see the route that you need to take, and the individual holds that you need to grasp. With patience and careful study, the route becomes obvious.

Planning, patience, focus and determination . . . the four cornerstones of a successful climb . . . of a successful life.

Climbers also know that once you start, you can't look back or second-guess the route you've chosen. Fear and self-doubt can kill. You just keep moving your limbs, trusting not only your instincts, but also in the care and planning that you put into choosing the route. Only then does the climb become a dance, a beautiful ballet of motion.

- Excerpt from *High Points: A Climber's Guide to Central America* by Jon Wunrow

The bizarre trend in mountaineers is not the risk they take, but the large degree to which they value life. They are not crazy because they don't dare, they are crazy because they do. These people tend to enjoy life to the fullest, laugh the hardest, travel the most, and work the least.

- Lisa Morgan

We must generate courage equal to the size of the difficulties we face.

- Dalai Lama

We are lucky whether we believe it or not.

- David Stevenson

People are used by twenty-four hours.
I use twenty-four hours.

- Chao-Chou

Climbers know that successful climbs and coming back
alive has a lot to do with careful planning, skill, endurance,
and keeping your head on straight, and even more to do
with luck. Any climber who has spent years in their pursuit
has also had their share of luck, and that alone is something
to be thankful for.

- Jon Wunrow

By dreaming about it, I was able to prepare myself for the
cold and desperate reality that followed. . . . It was indeed
magic to find that the initial commitment and inner strength
can bring you back down alive in the midst of such an
undertaking.

- Jonathan Waterman, on his 1982 winter ascent
of the Cassin Ridge, Denali

Climb if you will, but remember that courage and strength
are nothing without prudence, and that a momentary
negligence may destroy the happiness of a lifetime.

- Edward Whymper

*In mountaineering and exploration, efficiency does not
depend on the amassing of material and manpower, so
much as the power to improvise plans at a moment's
notice. In a word, to be adaptable. It is the opportunist who
is most successful in the Himalayas.*

- Frank S. Smythe

*Finish each day and be done with it.
You have done what you could.
Some blunders and absurdities no doubt crept in.
Forget them as soon as you can.
Tomorrow is a new day.
You shall begin it well and serenely.*

- Ralph Waldo Emerson

*To understand the heart and mind of a person, look not at
what he has already achieved, but what he aspires to do.*

- Khalil Gibran

But I do not believe in miracles.

- Reinhold Messner

*No, we are neither hard nor foolhardy; we shall never be
so. We are miserable, fearful rabbits who overcome our
fear, sometimes with a surge of courage, if it is really
necessary. . . . I never thought that I could muster so much
faith in myself after so much anxiety and despondency.*

- Reinhard Karl

41

I lose myself at some point during almost every musical performance. While I'm playing, there's a pattern of struggling through something and then cracking through it by a weird combination of willpower and letting go.

- David Torn

If you are not prepared to give a little credit to luck and chance, it would be better not to come to the Himalaya at all.

- G. Chevalley

Jump into experience while you are alive!
If you don't break your ropes while you are alive,
do you think ghosts will do it after?

- Kabir

THE BEAUTY OF NATURE

Adventurers who spend a lot of time adventuring end up spending a lot of time outdoors. Through the ages, extreme sports enthusiasts have talked and written about the intimate connection they feel to the rocks, waves, snow, and mountains that make up their playground. Some adventurers spend more intimate time with their physical surroundings than they do with people.

For me, part of climbing's allure is the opportunities it provides me to see and experience some of the most beautiful and awe-inspiring places on the planet. Words can't capture the feeling that comes with looking out the tent door across a glacier as the sun sets over a mountain ridge, or sitting next to the glassy reflection in a crystal clear alpine lake while thinking back on the day's adventure.

Even non-climbers who have stood at the base of Half

Dome or seen Bridal Veil Falls in the dead of winter, walked through a beautiful garden at a nearby park, or gotten up a little early to share a cup of coffee with the birds while sitting on the front porch swing don't have to ask about the connection that adventurers feel to nature— they've already felt it.

Nature is one of the few things in life that can deliver both brutality and death, and offer serenity and peace, depending on her mood or her whims. Nature can kill and nature can protect. She is a harsh and immediate teacher, and an understanding and patient mentor, often depending on what you are open to receiving and what she is in the mood to dole out. Spending time outdoors brings us more directly in contact with the consequences of our actions, as Robert Green Ingersoll wrote, "In nature there are neither rewards nor punishments; there are only consequences." Some of the best youth residential treatment programs for addictions and behavioral problems are programs that are based in the outdoors, with nature as the teacher of immediate, natural, and logical consequences. Risk takers and adventurers are well attuned to these kinds of consequences that stem directly from our actions.

Spending time close to nature, and away from the distractions and stresses of everyday life, allows those that are willing the opportunity to break through the barriers we create to understanding ourselves. Spending time outdoors gives us a fresh and uncluttered perspective, and helps us feel more centered and focused. I've often said that there is something very empowering about spending day after day moving through a harsh environment where the only things I need to think about are the weather, the route, food, water, safety, and how my body is responding to the conditions, things that put the rest of life in focus. There is a simplicity and an imminence that requires focusing on the moment and being attentive and present that offers a clarity that is harder to find apart from the natural world. Jack Kerouac said that spending time alone in nature helps us find ourselves, learn to depend on ourselves, and learn our true and inner strengths.

For most of us, the feelings that we experience when we spend time outdoors can't be put into words. Chuang-Tzu, a Chinese philosopher from the fourth century B.C., wrote, "The sound of water says what I think." So, I apologize in advance for trying to use my words, and the wise words of others like Jack Kerouac and Albert Einstein to attempt to capture some of what we experienced with nature.

Wind moving through the grass so the grass quivers. This moves me with an emotion that I don't even understand.

- Katherine Mansfield

Look deep into nature, and then you will understand everything better.

- Albert Einstein

Only in solitude do we find ourselves.

- Miguel de Unamuno

In the presence of eternity, the mountains are as transient as the clouds.

- Robert Green Ingersoll

Our father which art in heaven
Stay there
And we will stay on earth
Which is sometimes so pretty.

- Jacques Prevert

Everything in the universe has energy. All you have to do to access that energy is make it vibrate.

- John Wyer

Come into the mountains, dear friend.
Leave society and take no one with you but your true self.
Get close to nature.
Your everyday games will be insignificant.
Notice the clouds spontaneously forming patterns and try
to do that with your life.

- Susan Polis Schutz

It is good to know the truth, but it is better to speak of palm
trees.

- Arabic Proverb

One should not go into churches, if one wants to breath
pure air.

- Friedrich Nietzsche

To learn to see, to learn to hear, you must do this—go into
the wilderness alone.

- Don Jose

I never saw a wild thing feel sorry for itself.

- D.H. Lawrence

One touch of nature makes the whole world kin.

- William Shakespeare

When its over, I want to say: all my life,
I was a bride married to amazement.
I was the bridegroom, taking the world into my arms.

- Mary Oliver

Nirvana is right here, before our eyes.

- Hakuin

No man should go through life without once experiencing
healthy, even bored solitude in the wilderness, finding
himself depending solely on himself and thereby learning
his true and hidden strength.

- Jack Kerouac

Blow of an axe,
Pine scent,
The winter woods.

- Buson

To find the universal elements enough: to find the air and
the water exhilarating; to be refreshed by a morning walk or
an evening saunter . . . to be thrilled by the stars at night; to
be elated over a bird's nest or a wildflower in spring—these
are some of the rewards of the simple life.

- John Burroughs

If only we could pull out our brains and use only our eyes.

- Pablo Picasso

When the bird and the book disagree, always believe in the bird.

- John James Audobon

It is the top of the ninth inning. Man, always a threat at the plate, has been hitting nature hard. It is important to remember, however, that nature bats last.

- Paul Ehrlich

I came to realize that mind is no other than mountains and rivers and the great wide earth, the sun and the moon and the stars.

- Dogen

Come forth into the light of things. Let nature be your teacher.

- William Wordsworth

The goal of life is living in agreement with nature.

- Zeno

When one tugs at a single thing in nature, he finds it attached to the rest of the world.

- John Muir

People travel to wonder at the height of the mountains, at the huge waves of the sea, at the long course of rivers, at the vast compass of the ocean, at the circular motion of the stars; and they pass by themselves without wondering.

- St. Augustine

The ordinary man looking at a mountain is like an illiterate person confronted with a Greek manuscript.

- Aleister Crowley

One of the misfortunes of advancing age is that you get out of touch with the sunrise. You take it for granted, and it is over and done with before you settle yourself for the daily routine. That is one reason, I think, why when we grow older, the days seem shorter, we miss the high moments of their beginning.

- Lord Tweedmuir

Nature does not hurry, yet everything is accomplished.

- Lao-Tsu

As for me, I delight in the everyday Way,
Amongst mist-wrapped vines and rocky caves.
Here in the wilderness I am completely free,
With my friends, the white clouds, idling forever.
There are roads, but they do not reach my world.

- Han-Shan

BEING ATTENTIVE AND LIVING IN THE MOMENT

A long time ago, I read a book called *The Precious Present* by Spencer Johnson. I remember it as a short fable about the importance of acknowledging and appreciating the value of each moment, even in the midst of a fast-paced and complex world. We hear all the time that we should be focused on the moment and not worried about the future or the past. But why is it important to live in the moment? What does that kind of attentiveness look like in a practical sense, and why do risk takers seem to understand this concept better than most other people?

I can think of three reasons why living in the moment and being attentive are things that we should all espouse, or at least think about a bit more:

First, we live in a world of distractions. With a television on all evening long, iPhones, iPads, laptops, twenty-four-hour news cycles, hundreds of cable TV channels, texting, Twitter, Instant Messaging, and the like, we are constantly barraged with information that the generations before us never had, but we feel we can't live without. This deluge of information and distractions often serve to keep us focused on things outside of ourselves, outside of our control, and outside of the present moment. When we allow too many things to demand our attention it is easy to lose focus of the truly important things, and to be distracted by meaningless things.

If we can teach ourselves to be happy and at peace in this moment, we learn the secret of living a happy and content life. To do this, we need to create a space of inner calm in this moment and the next. Indira Gandhi wrote, "We must learn to be still in the midst of activity and to be vibrantly alive in repose." Surfers, climbers, skiers, and the like know that to be successful and to survive, it is important to purposefully seek and create this sense of inner calm in the midst of the terror and chaos that can come from taking great risks.

Second, this moment is all we really have. We simply cannot live in the past or the future. It's not possible. The past is gone and completely out of our control, and the future not only hasn't arrived yet, but it is not guaranteed. The future is also constantly changing based on what we do in the moment. The richness of life and the depth of our relationships are experienced in the moment, not in the past or the future. If we aren't paying attention, we miss them.

Henry Miller wrote, "The moment one gives close attention to any thing, even a blade of grass, it becomes a mysterious, awesome, indescribably magnificent world in itself." Again, extreme sports enthusiasts know exactly that Miller is talking about when it comes to skiers paying close attention to signs of avalanche risk, rock climbers paying close attention to the details of a vertical crack, or BASE jumpers paying very close attention to the nuances of a breeze. Engaging in this intense kind of focus can open up a whole new world of emotion and detail that others will never feel or experience. How often do we give this kind of close attention to our wife, to our son, to the strangers we come into contact with every day? Can you imagine the revolution in humankind that would take place if we used our "moments" to be truly attentive to the people who cross our path, to our enemies and not just our friends, and to those you have different views and beliefs than us? In his book *Zen and the Art of Motorcycle Maintenance,* Robert Pirsig wrote, "To live for some future goal is shallow. It is the sides of the mountains which sustain life, not the top." I'd add, that it's the attention we pay to the sides of the mountains that brings depth to our lives.

Finally, being attentive to the present moment allows us to live each day to the fullest. Knowing that this moment is all that we have encourages us to make the most of each moment. How does knowing that you could die tomorrow affect how you spend today and how you spend this moment? One thing I know for sure is that life is too short for all of us. The part of living that happens on Earth will come to an end for everyone reading this book. It may come tomorrow, or in forty years, but it will come, and most likely when you least expect it. So, the time to live is now. The time to love is now. The time to travel to new places is now. The time to risk is now. The time to say "I'm sorry" to someone you've hurt is now. The time to give away what you have to someone who needs it more is now. The time to pick up that piece of litter that you keep walking past is now. The time to hug your wife is now. The time to tell your son that you love him is now.

Risk takers understand the importance of being very attentive to everything that is happening in the moment. Climbers survive by living in the moment and paying close attention to the snow load on a ridge, to the very next hold on a rock face, to the lenticular clouds forming above the summit, and to the gurgle in their lungs at altitude. Surfers survive by focusing on the present wave in the present moment. Mountain bikers and skiers are completely focused on the bump or turn that is immediately in front of them. To focus on the past or the future when in the presence of a challenging and dangerous moment, can be fatal. The same can be said about life.

*The point is to perform every activity, from playing
basketball to taking out the garbage, with precise attention,
moment by moment.*

- Phil Jackson

*We're captive to the past and the future. We're so
distracted, and that's why a lot of people are unhappy. One
of the addictive aspects of climbing is that it allows you to
be in the present moment in ways that are impossible in
ordinary life.*

- Jim Wickwire

*If we act, in however small a way, we don't have to wait for
some grand utopian future. The future is an infinite
succession of presents, and to live now as we think human
beings should live, in defiance of all that is bad around us,
is itself a marvelous victory.*

- Howard Zinn

*Life, we learn too late, is in the living, in the tissue of every
day and hour.*

- Stephen Leacock

*Many eyes go through the meadow,
But few see the flowers in it.*

- Ralph Waldo Emerson

March gone. Now, April's moon. I age: how many more to meet?
Won't let mind linger on the endless things beyond me.
I'll try to finish this one small cup.

- Tu Fu

The butterfly counts not days but moments,
And has time enough.

- Rabindranath Tagore

Life is precious, and it's happening now.

- Les Schlick

Nothing is worth more than this day.

- Goethe

TODAY.

- *Word carved on a stone on*
John Ruskin's Desk

"I wish it need not have happened in my time," said Frodo.
"So do I," said Gandalf, "and so do all who live to see such
times. But that is not for them to decide. All we have to
decide is what to do with the time that is given us."

- Excerpt from *The Fellowship of the Ring*
by J.R.R. Tolkien

Normally, we do not so much look at things as overlook them.

- Alan Watts

There is one art, no more, no less. To do all things with artlessness.

- Piet Hein

The moment when life is now, without past or future, beyond earthly mundanities, is an intoxicating state.

- Maria Coffey

Life it too short to be in a hurry.

- Henry David Thoreau

There is no end. There is no beginning. There is only the infinite passion of life.

- Federico Fellini

Well, what I learned in Chile is that we are never more alone than when we are on our computers or stuck in traffic, and we are never more connected than when we are present where we are. And it is impossible not to be present in a place like Patagonia.

- Mason Jennings

This is the moment. You have no other moment.

- Jon Wunrow

Each night, when I go to sleep, I die. And the next morning, when I wake up,
I am reborn.

- Mahatma Gandhi

Right now a moment of time is passing by! . . . We must become that moment.

- Paul Cezanne

If you love someone, tell him. If you have a gift to give . . . give it now. Just in case.

- Maria Coffey

Better than a hundred years lived in idleness and in weakness is a single day of life lived with courage and powerful striving.

- The Dhammapada

Seize from the moment its unique novelty.

- André Gide

Each second is a universe of time.

- Henry Miller

Each day should be passed as though it were our last.

- Publilius Syrus

*Our mind should be free from traces of the past,
Just like flowers in spring.*

- Shunryu Suzuki

*Let other people go into trances and think about
spirituality. I'd rather concentrate on having something to
eat. The here and now.*

- Gene Simmons, lead singer
for the band KISS

*Don't move. Just die over and over. Don't anticipate.
Nothing can save you now, because this is our last moment.
Not even enlightenment will help you now, because you
have no other moments. With no future, be true to
yourself—and don't move.*

- Shunryu Suzuki, to his
students in the zendo

Existence begins in every instant.

- Friedrich Nietzsche

*Today I will think about the tasks and rewards of this day.
And trust the future for what is unanswered.*

- Unknown

Time is not a line, but a series of now points.

- Taisen Deshimaru

*I've stopped thinking all the time of what happened
yesterday. And stopped asking myself what's going to
happen tomorrow. What's happening today, this minute,
that's what I care about. I say: What are you doing at this
moment Zorba? . . . I'm kissing a woman. Well, kiss her
well, Zorba! And forget all the rest while you're doing it;
there's nothing else on earth, only you and her!*

- Nikos Kazantzakis

And don't forget—forever is always now.

- Josh Baran

*It's hard work being hopeful. . . . I just say my prayers
everyday and always thank God for people who are not
only aware but active out there . . . keep your eyes (and
heart) wide open.*

- Stephen Wunrow

Appreciate the moment. Don't fear the future.

- Unknown

Be content in the moment, and be willing to follow the flow. Then there will be no room for grief or joy.

- Chuang-Tzu

There is no murder worse than the killing of time.

- Yamamoto Gempo Roshi

The present never ages. Each moment is like a snowflake, unique, unspoiled, unrepeatable, and can be appreciated in its surprisingness.

- Gail Sheehy

The point of life is always arrived at in the immediate moment.

-Alan Watts

Renew thyself completely each day; do it again, and again, and forever again.

- Chinese Saying

Do all your work as if you had a thousand years to live and as if you know you must die tomorrow.

- Mother Anne Lee, Shaker Founder

ACCEPTANCE AND BEING CONTENT

We live in a competitive world. We live in a material world. We live in a fast-paced and demanding world. Our human nature compels us to constantly compare ourselves to others—what they own, what they look like, how much money they have, how their kids behave. Extreme sports enthusiasts are in constant competition with themselves and others to risk more, climb higher, dive deeper—bigger, better, faster, riskier. Finding ways to be content, and to be thankful for what we have and who we are is a challenge even to the most saintly and spiritually evolved among us.

In seeking contentment, there is a balance between action and inaction, between getting things done and leaving things undone, between accepting what is and fighting for what should be. Finding this balance is downright tough, and for adventurers who are often busy seeking the next rush, it can be even tougher. There are no rules and few guidelines when it comes to feeling content, because the state of contentedness is as individual as our fingerprints. I may be content in constant movement and you may be content in constant repose. When each of us seeks a state of contentment, we all need to find our own balance between action and inaction. Zen Master Shunryu Suzuki summarized the art of acceptance and being content when he wrote, "Each of you is perfect the way you are . . . and you can use a little improvement."

My guess is that most risk takers and adventurers have a hard time feeling content, believing that the effort they made was good enough, that the summit they failed to reach wasn't meant to be climbed that trip, or that the big wave they sought never showed up this time out. I have spent three weeks attempting to climb Mt. Logan, the highest peak in Canada, three different times. The first time, we got to about 17,000 feet and after several days up high, in minus thirty-degree temperatures, we just couldn't find our way through the crevasses to the summit plateau. The second time I went with the intent of climbing nearby King Peak, and afterwards grabbing Logan's summit as well, but after a scary and unsuccessful attempt on King Peak, the last thing I felt like doing was hanging around for another two weeks to go for Logan's summit. The third time I went to Mt. Logan, we spent several days trapped in a blizzard at 17,000 feet and then watched as several experienced climbers were rescued off the summit plateau by a military helicopter just above us after the climbers had spent the same blizzard in an exposed bivouac. Two days later we crossed the huge summit plateau and climbed to the top of Logan's West Peak, but didn't have the energy or will to continue to the actual summit only one hundred feet higher. Three times to Mt. Logan, and three times I failed to get to the true summit. Do I feel content? Am I content with the effort I made? The simple answer is no, I don't feel content about just leaving this piece of unfinished mountaineering business and moving on. I already have a date in mind for my fourth attempt. So where is the balance? How do I find a feeling of contentedness?

Another facet of being content has to do with acceptance. Acceptance is an understanding or acknowledgement of things as they are in this moment. Acceptance is an eyes-wide-open awareness of the way things are as they appear to us. Daito Kokushi, thirteenth century Zen Master, took acceptance to an even more life changing level when he wrote the following:

> *No umbrella,*
> *getting soaked,*
> *I'll use the rain as my raincoat.*

Zen Master Kokushi takes the concept of acceptance beyond contentment and into the realm of reshaping our "negative" circumstances into something positive and even protective. Accepting things as they are is very different from allowing them to remain that way. Don't confuse acceptance with acquiescence, inertia, or surrender. There are times in our lives when acceptance is cause for inaction, and there are times when taking action is the only way to accept a situation and move on. Whether you are a spiritual person, an adrenaline junky, an addict, or none of the above, the Serenity Prayer of Alcoholics Anonymous, gives us some very helpful guidance when finding that line between acceptance through inaction, and acceptance through action: "God grant me the serenity to accept the things I can not change, the courage to change the things I can, and the wisdom to know the difference."

Yesterday I went on a little hike with my nephews and niece. While we were on the hike, all of the sudden Isaac says, "You know what days I love? I love it when you get up early and eat breakfast then go to school and come home and watch cartoons then eat dinner and go to bed." I laughed so hard and then said, "Isaac, that is every day!" Then it dawned on me that the kid is on to something. How cute. Enjoy every day! I think he is a budding Buddhist.

- Leslie Skooglund

I used to think that someday I'd be able to resolve the different drives I have in different directions, the tension between the different people that I am. Now I realize that is who I am, and I'm more content to be discontent.

- Bono, singer for the band U2

Men spend their lives worrying about things that never happen.

- Moliere

What a wonderful life I've had! I only wish I'd realized it sooner.

- Colette

He who knows he has enough is rich.

- Tao Te Ching

I'm erecting a barrier of simplicity between myself and the world.

- Andre Gide

Maybe true. Maybe not true. Better you believe.

- Sherpa Saying

To the right, books; to the left, a tea cup.
In front of me, the fireplace; behind me, the post.
There is no greater happiness than this.

- Teiga

All the way to heaven is heaven.

- St. Catherine of Siena

My advice to you is not to inquire why or whither but just enjoy your ice cream while it's on your plate.

- Thornton Wilder

Just simply alive,
        both of us,
                I and the poppy.

- Issa

*There was a beautiful young girl who became pregnant out
of wedlock, and told her angry parents that the father was
an old and revered Zen master with a reputation for living a
pure life. When the angry parents accused the master, all
he said was, "Is that so?" After the child was born, the
master brought the baby into his house and raised it as his
own. After a year passed, the girl, stricken with remorse,
finally recanted and told her parents that the master was
entirely innocent. The embarrassed parents came to fetch
the child, apologizing to the master and begging his
forgiveness. All he said was, "Is that so?"*

- Zen Story

*All of us are apprenticed to the same teacher—reality. It is
as hard to get the children herded into the car pool and
down the road to the bus as it is to chant sutras in the
Buddha-hall on a cold morning. One is not better than the
other; each can be quite boring; and they both have the
virtuous quality of repetition. Repetition and its good results
make the very activities of our life into the path.*

- Gary Snyder

*Sit, rest, work. Alone with yourself, never weary. On the
edge of the forest, live joyfully, without desire.*

- The Buddha

*The lost child,
 Crying, crying,
  But still catching fireflies.*

- Ryusui

Surely joy is the condition of life.

- Henry David Thoreau

My old wife draws a board for chess.
My son bends pins for fishhooks.
I'm often sick, but I can find good herbs.
What, beyond this, could a simple man ask?

- Tu Fu

You owe it to everyone (including yourself) to find pockets
of tranquility in your busy world.

- George Bernanos

Who can be a wild deer
Among deserted mountains
Happy with grass and pines.

- Han-shan

Be content where you are.
Nothing more.
Nothing less.

- Unknown

There is no such thing as bad weather, only inappropriate
clothing.

- Ranulph Fiennes

71

Besides the noble art of getting things done, there is the noble art of leaving things undone. The wisdom of life consists in the elimination of nonessentials.

- Lin Yutang

The morning after the storm
The melons alone
Know nothing of it.

- Sodo

It isn't the burdens of today that drive men mad. It is the regrets over yesterday and the fear of tomorrow. Regret and fear are twin thieves who rob us of today.

- Unknown

If the only prayer you ever say in your entire life is "thank you," it will be enough.

- Meister Eckhart

My bed is small, but I rest at ease,
My clothes are thin, but my body is warm,
My food is scarce, but I am nourished.

- Milarepa

Paradise is where I am.

- Francois-Marie Voltaire

Painful it is indeed,
Passing through the world;
But in a hovel like this,
I live on in peace and quiet,
Winter rain falling.

- Nijoin Sanuki

If enlightenment is not where you are standing, where will
you look?

- Zen Saying

A pleasant and happy life does not come from external
things. People must draw from within themselves, as from a
spring, pleasure and joy.

- Plutarch

To enjoy the world without judgment is what a realized life
is like.

- Charlotte Joko Beck

There is no heaven nor earth,
Only snow,
Falling incessantly.

- Hashin

Just to be alive is enough.

- Shunryu Suzuki

There is a time for work. And a time for love. That leaves no other time.

- Coco Chanel

You are already complete. You just don't know it.

- Seung Sahn

"He insulted me, he harmed me, he robbed me, he beat me." If you think like this, you will suffer. "He insulted me, he harmed me, he robbed me, he beat me." If you do not think like this, you will not suffer.

- Anonymous

When we are unable to find tranquility within ourselves, it is useless to seek it elsewhere.

- La Rochefoucauld

If the mind is tranquil and occupied with positive thoughts, the body will not easily fall prey to disease.

- Dalai Lama

If you understand, things are just as they are;
If you do not understand, things are just as they are.

- Zen Verse

The place you are right now God circled on a map for you.

- Ibraham Hafiz

If you can spend a perfectly useless afternoon in a perfectly useless manner, you have learned how to live.

- Lin Yu-T'ang

But I still haven't found what I'm looking for.

- Lyrics of "Still Haven't Found
What I'm Looking For" by U2

Mid-life seems to have snuck up on us, but it turns out to be a darn good time of life. We get to finally practice being ourselves, some of which is fun.

- Les Schlick

Freedom from the desire for an answer is essential to the understanding of the problem.

- Krishnmurti

Learn to wish that everything should come to pass exactly as it does.

- Epictetus

Right now, at this very moment, we have a mind, which is all the basic equipment we need to achieve complete happiness.

- Howard Cutler

If there is to be any peace, it will come through being, not having.

- Henry Miller

When hungry, eat your rice.
When tired, close your eyes.

- Lin-Chi

Let us try to recognize the precious nature of each day.

- The 14ᵗʰ Dalai Lama

The greatest part of our happiness and disappointments are a result of our dispositions and not our circumstances.

- Martha Washington

The truth is that we were all very, very lucky.

- Marc Twight

Thank God for the things I do not own.

- St. Teresa of Avila

Nothing is left to you at this moment but to have a good laugh.

- Zen Saying

Every day is a special day. Every place is a special place as it is.

- Bernie Glassman

The interesting thing about greed is that although the underlying motive is to seek satisfaction, even after obtaining the object of one's desire, one is still not satisfied. On the other hand, if one has a strong sense of contentment, it doesn't matter whether one obtains the object or not; either way, one is still content.

- Dalai Lama

This is a world of action, and not for moping and groaning in.

- Charles Dickens

You are already complete. You just don't know it.

- Zen Saying

I am walking barefoot over pebbles in the swift creek, its gurgling sound delights my ear while soft spring wind moves my robe. These are things that make life happy.

-Han Yu

To get this chance is very difficult. To be born as a human being is very difficult. Among uncountable sperms and eggs . . . you are here. Wonderful chance. Congratulations!

- Soen Nakagawa

Kindness is more important than wisdom, and the recognition of this is the beginning of wisdom.

- Theodore Rubin

Learn to be calm and you will always be happy.

- Paramhansa Yogananda

When passing a neutral person in a crowd, think: this person does not seem to have any relation to me in this lifetime, but over the continuum of lives has definitely been my mother, father, child, or closest friend. In this way you will slowly develop the feeling that all sentient beings are your friends.

- Dalai Lama

From the first, in people and things, there is no such thing as trash.

- Zuigan Roshi

The fact is, the universe has chosen you as the vehicle through which to experience the uncanny thrill of cutting up cabbage for dinner, the wonder that is inhaling oxygen and exhaling carbon dioxide, the fabulous spectacle of watching your clothes dry at a coin-op laundromat where the radio is stuck on an E-Z listening station and an old lady keeps staring at you for no discernible reason. The universe has demanded that you be you. Ain't no avoidin' it.

- Brad Warner

If the horse is dead . . . dismount.

- John Holst

CLEAR MIND

The Buddhist concept of emptiness, or clear mind, has always been a tough one for me to grasp. Most quotes in this short section are from Zen masters and Buddhists like the Dalai Lama—people who have spent their lifetime practicing and occasionally trying to explain the concept of emptying the mind. Over the years, I've read a lot of these Buddhist teachings and have saved a number of Buddhist quotes. Still, a basic understanding of the concept evades me, probably because I'm thinking too hard and not focusing on actually clearing my mind of the clutter. I'm trying to use the constructs that have been built up in my mind over the years to make sense of something that is outside the realm of mental constructs. I've tried to use words to describe something that was represented by the absence of words, as Edward Dahlberg once wrote, "It

81

takes a long time to understand nothing." So rather than try to explain, I'll let the quotes do it for me, and for you.

I know that there is a connection between being able to empty my mind and being good at climbing, or at any extreme sport. I can feel it, but I'm not sure I can explain it. Clearing one's mind to focus on a single thought, on a single mantra, on nothing, is much like clearing one's mind to focus on the next climbing move, gasping for the next breath at altitude, psyching up for the next snowboard run, or the next big wave. The ability to block out all other thoughts, fears, and distractions to maintain a single focus— in essence to focus on nothing—takes a lot of practice, but its something we all can learn to do.

The quieter you become, the more you can hear.

> - Baba Ram Dass

Whenever I start working on a song, I immediately try to forget everything, to empty my hands and head of anything that may be hanging over from another song or album. I try to approach it like, "This is the first time I've ever played a guitar. What am I going to do?"

> - The Edge, guitarist from the band U2

Sometimes nothin's a pretty cool hand.

> - Cool Hand Luke

Muddy water is best cleared by leaving it alone.

> - Alan Watts

When chanting, or sitting, or bowing, even special practicing cannot help you if you are attached to your thinking. Taoist chanting, Confucian chanting, Christian chanting, Buddhist chanting don't matter. Chanting "Coca Cola, Coca Cola, Coca Cola . . ." can be just as good if you keep a clear mind. But if you don't keep a clear mind, and are only following your thinking as you mouth the words, even the Buddha cannot help you.

> - Soen Sa Nim

Our minds are continually active, fabricating and anxious, creating a self-preoccupied veil which partially conceals the world.

- Iris Murdoch

The game is not about becoming somebody, it's about becoming nobody.

- Baba Ram Dass

The corn will not grow unless we start the year with a good mind.

- Ancient Hopi Belief

Any fool can be fussy and rid himself of energy all over the place, but a man has to have something in him before he can settle down and do nothing.

- J.B. Priestley

Beware of the people who have known solitude. They're dangerous. They march to a different drum beat.

- Loren Halvorsen

Just keep clear mind, go straight ahead, try, try, try for ten thousand years.

- Soen Sa Nim

*Some of us need to discover that we will not begin to
live more fully until we have the courage to do and see and
taste and experience much less than usual. . . .*

*There are times, then, when in order to keep ourselves
in existence at all we simply have to sit back for a while and
do nothing. And for a man who has let himself be drawn
completely out of himself by his activity, nothing is more
difficult than to sit still and rest doing nothing at all.*

*The very act of resting is the hardest and most
courageous act he can perform.*

- Thomas Merton

Don't just do something. Sit there!

- Thich Nhat Hanh

*To live without emotion, hope, or aim.
In the presence of my cottage fire.
And listen to the flapping of the flame,
Or kettle whispering its faint undersong.*

- William Wordsworth

*When no thought arises, is there still any fault? Mount
Everest!*

- Zen Saying

What you see with your eyes closed is what counts.

- Lame Deer, Lakota Sage

If it rains, let it rain.
If wind blows, let it blow.

- Ikkyu

It is our mind, and that alone, that chains us or sets us free.

- Dilgo Khyentse Rinpoche

I fear nothing, I hope for nothing, I am free.

- Nikos Kazantzakis

Lose your mind and come to your senses.

- Fritz Perls

A permanent state of transition is man's most noble
condition.

- Juan Ramon Jimenez

FINDING YOUR PATH IN LIFE

One thing that we all have in common is that at one point or at many points during our lives, we are all trying to find our way in this world. Whether it is in adolescence and early adulthood when we are clarifying our identity and future vocation, or during mid-life when we aren't where we thought we'd be or with the person we thought we'd be with. It may even be in our senior years when we wonder whether there are still ways for us to make an impact and be of value in this world.

Adolescents, job hunters, spiritual seekers, college students, and middle-aged men all seek a roadmap to follow into the future, and a lens through which we can

87

focus our past experiences and frame our decision making. Steven Tyler, front man of the band Aerosmith, said, "We're all bozos on a bus until we find a way to express ourselves." Tyler's means of self-expression, of course, is music. Some people find their direction and means of self-expression in a particular religion. Some use their vocation and career as the way to define themselves and provide direction for their path forward. Some of us use risk taking as a way to define ourselves. Yet others are wanderers who, rather than choose their path, often let their path chose them and then change directions based on what they encounter along the way.

How do you know which life paths to take, whether making small decisions or ones that seem monumental? Do you take the easiest and most comfortable route? Or do you take the road less traveled, hoping that it will make all the difference? Do you make risky decisions? Do you follow your gut? Do you follow your heart? Do you leap before you look? Do you follow your friend's or your family's advice and remain oblivious to your heart's desire? Do you follow social convention or make the decision that most other people would make? Or do you wait so long to make a tough decision that it ultimately gets made for you as the other options disappear?

In trying to find your path, ask yourself a few questions: What is it that you are passionate about? What do you love to do? What makes you smile? What motivates you to get up in the morning? If you aren't sure about the answers to these questions, don't worry about it or put pressure on yourself. Plenty of us have spent a good part of our lives being unsure of these answers. But if you aren't sure, then take some time to explore these simpler, less complex questions: What kinds of people do you enjoy being around? What can you do to make the world, or just the street you're walking down, a better place? What can you do to make the person sitting next to you smile? What's one thing that you can do today that will reduce the suffering in this world by just a little tiny bit? Answering any one of these questions can help you start to find your path.

For me, I'm beginning to learn that defining the ultimate goals and paths for my life is less important than focusing on the things that are happening along the way. It is so easy to get hung up on trying to find the perfect job or career, or making sure you make the right decision about what school to attend or what your major should be. Don't misunderstand, goals can be important motivators and direction setters, but focusing too much on goals and endpoints can cause a lot of unneeded misery along the way. Life gets lived in a series of moments and the actions we take in those moments. The only control we really have in this world is over what we chose to do in this moment.

Successful business owner, ice and mountain climbing pioneer, and global environmentalist Yvon Chouinard surely has set lots of goals in his life, but even he once said, "It's kinda like the quest for the holy grail. Who gives a shit about what the grail is. It's the quest that matters." It's the quest that matters. It's the seeking and exploring and risking and attempting that matters. For me, the key to living a self-directed life, and finding one's path, is being willing to make mistakes and to try something knowing that you might fail. You must be willing to fall down and get back up and fall down and get back up again. Risk takers and adventurers understand these things.

The fear of making a mistake or of making the "wrong" choice can be paralyzing for some. Often the biggest barrier to making a decision is our fear of the unknowns that will follow, and of messing something up if we try, or of facing the reality that the path we've been on may no longer be the right one or the best one for us. In light of this concept, our friend Chouinard also said that "sometimes progress involves making a 180-degree turn, and then taking one step forward."

Ultimately, the quest for purpose, for finding our path in life is a personal journey. There is a Zen saying that goes,

"If you are born clumsy it's not bad. If you are born clever it's not good. The proper way to serve tea is to find your own way." In other words, finding your own way in this life is not based on the traits that we were born with, or the station in life that we were handed. The only "right" path to follow—in other words, the only proper way to serve tea—is to find our own way, and then make that the right way. This wisdom is echoed by Poet Antonio Machado who wrote, "Traveler, there is no path. You make your path as you travel."

What's holding you back? What's keeping you from living a life full of possibility? What's keeping you from choosing a path, and then taking one step in that direction?

Twenty years from now, you'll be more disappointed by the things you didn't do than by the ones you did. So throw off the bowlines, sail away from the safe harbor, catch the trade winds in your sails. Explore. Dream. Discover.

- Mark Twain

Do or do not. There is not try.

- Yoda

When I am busy with little things, I am not required to do greater things.

- St. Francis de Sales

Without the rocket, we're just another dysfunctional family.

- *The Astronaut Farmer*, Film, 2006

The race will go to the curious, the slightly mad and those with an unsated passion for learning and daredevilry.

- Tom Peters

We often struggle with making the right decision. I've learned over the years, that there are very few "wrong" choices. Life is about taking the risk to make a decision, and then doing everything within your power to make it the right decision.

- Jon Wunrow

It's okay to do the work you want to do, until the time comes to do the work you were meant to do.

- The Rookie, Film, 2002

This is what you shall do: Love the earth and sun and the animals, despise riches, give alms to everyone that asks, and stand up for the stupid and crazy.

- Walt Whitman

We should tackle reality in a slightly joking way . . . otherwise we miss its point.

- Lawrence Durrell

Listen to your life. See it for the fathomless mystery that it is. In the boredom and pain of it no less than the excitement and gladness: Touch, taste, smell your way to the holy and hidden part of it, because in the last analysis all moments are key moments, and life itself is grace.

- Frederick Buechner

The purpose of life is not to be happy. It is to be useful, to be honorable, to be compassionate, to have it make some difference that you have lived and lived well.

- Ralph Waldo Emerson

A mistake proves that someone stopped talking long enough to do something.

- Unknown

A perfection of means and confusion of aims seems to be our main problem.

- Albert Einstein

I would love to live as the river flows, carried by the surprise of its own unfolding.

- John O'Donohue

If you wish to know the road up the mountain, you must ask the man who goes back and forth on it.

- Zen Saying

Today, like every other day, we wake up empty and frightened. Don't open the door to the study and begin reading. Take down a musical instrument.
Let the beauty we love be what we do.

- Rumi, 11th Century Sufi Poet

You cannot teach a man anything. You can only help him find it within himself.

- Socrates

Life without purpose is merely existence.

- Unknown

The truth is where the truth is, and it's sometimes in the candy store.

- Bob Dylan

To a worm inside a horseradish, the whole world is horseradish.

- Yiddish Proverb

Eliminate something superfluous from your life. Break a habit. Do something that makes you feel insecure. Carry out an action with complete attention and intensity, as if it were your last.

- Piero Ferrucci

The simplest things give me ideas.

-Joan Miró

It is good to have an end to journey towards; but it is the journey that matters, in the end.

- Ursula K. Le Guin

A painting of a rice cake does not satisfy hunger.

- Zen Saying

One sees great things from the valley;
Only small things from the peak.

- G.K. Chesterton

Never let the odds keep you from doing what you know in
your heart you were meant to do.

- H. Jackson Brown, Jr.

Climbing . . . is a useless sport. You get to be a
conquistador of the useless. You climb to the summit and
there is nothing there. . . . How you get there is the
important part.

- Yvon Chouinard

Paths cannot be taught, they can only be taken.

- Zen Saying

Go confidently in the direction of your dreams. Live the
life you've imagined.

- Henry David Thoreau

May your trails be crooked, winding, lonesome, dangerous, leading to the most amazing view. May your mountains rise into and above the clouds.

- Edward Abbey

If we have not found heaven within, it is a certainty we will not find it without.

- Henry Miller

The road uphill and the road downhill are one and the same.

- Heraclitus

Many men go fishing all their lives without knowing that it is not fish they are after.

- Henry David Thoreau

I embrace emerging experience. I participate in discovery. I am a butterfly. I am not a butterfly collector. I want the experience of the butterfly.

- William Stafford

It's not the answer that enlightens, but the question.

- Eugene Ionesco

I have learned to have very modest goals for society and myself, things like clean air, green grass, children with bright eyes, not being pushed around, useful work that suits one's abilities, plain tasty food. . . .

- Paul Goodman

A society grows great when old men plant trees whose shade they know they will never sit in.

- Greek Proverb

If I had my life to live over, I would relax more. I wouldn't take so many things so seriously. I would take more chances, and climb more mountains, and swim more rivers. Next time, I'd start barefooted earlier in the Spring and stay that way later in the Fall. I wouldn't make such good grades unless I enjoyed working for them. I'd go to more dances. I'd ride more merry-go-rounds. I'd pick more daisies.

- Frank Dickey

For I have said that the medium of some men is paint or stone or a boat or a schoolroom, or poems or paper and ink; that of a few is rocks and snow and the upward moving of limbs.

- Wilfrid Noyce

To know the road ahead, ask those coming back.

- Chinese Proverb

Zazen isn't about blissing out or going into an alpha brainwave trance. It's about facing who and what you really are, in every single goddamn moment.

- Brad Warner

I'm just an ant on a log. I'm not rowing the fucking boat. It ain't "me," it's "us." I am a control freak, but I'm definitely an "us" kind of guy. The meaning of life for Glenn Hughes is to survive and lead a purposeful life.

- Glenn Hughes, formerly of bands
Deep Purple and Trapeze

Finish every day and be done with it. You have done what you could. Some blunders and absurdities crept in. Forget them as soon as you can. Tomorrow is a new day; you should begin it serenely and with too high a spirit to be encumbered with your old nonsense.

- Ralph Waldo Emerson

Become the change you want to see in others.

- Mahatma Ghandi

If you don't know what you want, it's harder to get it.

- Malcolm Forbes

Today there is no wind to hold me back. Today there is no wind to push me. Today I go on my own strength.

- Robert Davidson

Learn the rules, so you know how to break them properly.

- Unknown

Giving is the secret of a healthy life . . . not necessarily money, but whatever a man has, of encouragement and sympathy and understanding.

- John D. Rockefeller

There simply isn't time to waste.

- Unknown

To be surprised, to wonder, is to begin to understand.

- Jose Ortega y Gasset

Make your work your play and your play your work.

- Phil Jackson

There are years that ask questions. And years that answer.

- Excerpt from *Their Eyes Were Watching God* by Zora Neale Hurston

Thou shalt love life more than the meaning of life.

- Feodor Dostoyevsky

If your life is too complex, narrow your path a little.

- Unknown

*If your compassion does not include yourself, it is
incomplete.*

- Jack Kornfield

*Life and death are of supreme importance.
Time passes swiftly and opportunity is lost.
Let us awaken. Do not squander your life.*

- Zen Evening Chant

*Shaggy hair past the ears,
A worn out robe resembling white clouds and dark smoke.
Half drunk, half sober, I return home.
Children all around, guiding me along the way.*

- Ryokan

*All human beings should try to learn before they die what
they are running from, and to, and why.*

- James Thurber

Few will have the greatness to bend history itself; but each of us can work to change a small portion of events, and on the total of all those acts will be written the history of this generation.

- John F. Kennedy

Simplifying our lives does not mean sinking into idleness, but on the contrary, getting rid of the most subtle aspect of laziness: the one which makes us take on thousands of less important activities.

- Matthieu Ricard

If I meet a hundred-year-old man and I have something to teach him, I will teach; if I meet an eight-year-old boy and he has something to teach me, I will learn.

- Chao-Chou

You can't talk yourself out of something that you've behaved yourself into.

- Steven Covey

You can avoid reality. But you can't avoid the consequences of reality.

- Ayn Rand

The more we live by intellect, the less we understand the meaning of life.

- Leo Tolstoy

And so I urge you: go after experience rather than knowledge. Knowledge may often deceive you, but experience can not deceive you.

- Excerpt from *The Cloud of Unknowing*, anonymous work of 14th century Christian mysticism

The great end of life is not knowledge but action.

- Thomas Henry Huxley

There is no reality except the one contained within us. That is why so many people live such an unreal life. They take the images outside of them for reality and never allow the world within to assert itself.

- Hermann Hesse

Let your passion define your path.

- Unknown

In the end, everything is a gag.

- Charlie Chaplin

*Life is too short and I was just thinking this evening about
how I really and truly want to live. First of all, I want a good
cup of coffee every morning and a glass of wine every night.
I want to spend as much time as I can with the people I
love the most and I want to feel fulfilled in whatever I do. I
want to help as many people as I can, have fun, relax, take
care of my body, and make each day something to
remember even if just in a tiny way. Oh, and if I could add
one thing . . . I'd shop more.*

- Leslie Skooglund

If only I may grow:
Firmer
Simpler
Quieter
Warmer.

- Dag Hammarskjold

*If your philosophy doesn't grow corn, I don't want to hear
about it.*

- Sun Bear

*My sole desire is to live creatively in the present; in a
balance of contentment and anticipation.*

- Jon Wunrow

One day a student of the great Master Nasrudin passes by his house and finds the master on his knees rummaging in the grass. "What are you looking for, sir?"

"I'm looking for my key."

"But sir, didn't you lose it in your house?"

"Yes," says Nasrudin, "but there's more light out here."

- Sufi Tale

The real voyage of discovery consists not in seeking new landscapes, but in having new eyes.

- Marcel Proust

The challenge remains. On the other side are formidable forces: money, political power, the major media. On our side are the people of the world and a power greater than money or weapons: the truth. Truth has a power of its own. Art has a power of its own. That age-old lesson—that everything we do matters—is the meaning of the people's struggle here in the United States and everywhere. A poem can inspire a movement. A pamphlet can spark a revolution. Civil disobedience can arouse people who provoke us to think.

- Howard Zinn

This is the ultimate fact: "I am here."

- Shunryu Suzuki

An adult is one who has lost the grace, the freshness, the innocence of the child, who is no longer capable of feeling pure joy, who makes everything complicated, who spreads suffering everywhere, who is afraid of being happy, and who, because it is easier to bear, has gone back to sleep. The wise man is a happy child.

- Arnaud Desjardins

The art of being wise is the art of knowing what to overlook.

- William James

Whatever you can do, or dream you can, begin it. Boldness has genius, power and magic in it.

- Goethe

I arise in the morning torn between a desire to improve the world and a desire to enjoy the world. This makes it hard to plan the day.

- E.B. White

BEING OPEN TO THE POSSIBLE

Adventurers are dreamers of a sort. They look at a mountain peak and imagine a route. They see a far off wave and wonder if they can surf it. They push their physical and psychological limits to follow a dream of doing something they've never done before. They imagine completing a sequence of moves, or runs, or routes, over and over in their mind, long before their body follows the path that their mind imagined.

When spending lots of time in a natural environment where variables like weather, motivation, and snow conditions can and do change without notice, being open to other options, and weighing the consequences, becomes an important and sometimes lifesaving frame of mind.

107

The important thing about options is knowing that in almost every situation, we have them—no matter how dire, or scary, or hopeless our situation seems. Knowing we have options gives us hope. I've said it so many times to people—to kids who have made mistakes and are now facing legal consequences, to peers stuck in dead-end jobs who don't dare quit because they need the money, to friends who feel trapped in unsatisfying relationships, but are too scared to leave—that often the simple act of identifying options helps us feel less stuck, less trapped, and more in control of our situation.

The hardest part of "being open to the possible" is resisting that initial and often pervasive thought that the option(s) we've come up with won't work. We spend so much time and energy convincing ourselves that something won't work or just isn't possible that we stop dreaming. We stop imagining. We give up. We narrow our definition of what's possible, and keep reinforcing our stuckness. We create a belief system that we don't have options, that we just can't change our situation, and then we set about reinforcing the myth. We forget how to dream.

Opportunities come to us when we open ourselves up to them, as H. Jackson Brown, Jr. said, "opportunity dances with those on the dance floor." But you have to have the courage and determination to step onto the dance floor of life's opportunities. Maybe that's why we take the risks that we take, because it's our dance floor of opportunities. Do you dwell in a world of certainties, or in a world of possibilities?

I dwell in possibility.

- Emily Dickinson

We must listen to our hopes rather then our fears.

- Barack Obama

Learning to live is learning to let go.

- Sogyal Rinpoceh

Luke: I can't believe it.
Yoda: This is why you fall.

- *Star Wars: Episode V*, Film, 1980

Change is mandatory. Growth is optional.

- Unknown

I can scarcely wait till tomorrow
When a new life begins for me
As it does each day,
As it does each day.

- Stanley Kunitz

*Some men see things as they are, and ask why?
I dream things that never were and ask, why not?*

- Robert Kennedy

You can not depend on your eyes when your imagination is out of focus.

- Unknown

We are more curious about the meaning of dreams than about things we see when awake.

- Diogenes

The world as it is, just won't do. We have an obligation to fight for the world as it should be.

- Michelle Obama

Remember that not getting what you want is sometimes a wonderful stroke of luck.

- Dalai Lama

We do not have to accept a situation we can not bare. We have the power to change it.

- Barack Obama

Behind all this, some great happiness is hiding.

- Yehuda Amichai

The day is coming when a single carrot, freshly observed, will set off a revolution.

- Paul Cézanne

When we realize the everlasting truth of "everything changes," and find our composure in it, we find ourselves in nirvana.

- Shunryu Suzuki

Good fortune is not permanent; consequently, it is dangerous to become too attached to things going well.

- Dalai Lama

Sometimes, if you stand on the bottom rail of a bridge and lean over to watch the river slipping away beneath you, you suddenly know everything there is to be known.

- Winnie the Pooh, in
A. A. Milne's *Winnie the Pooh*

In three words I can sum up everything I've learned about life. It goes on.

- Robert Frost

*Nothing is secure but life, transition, the energizing spirit. . .
People wish to be settled; but only so far as they are
unsettled is there any hope for them.*

- Ralph Waldo Emerson

*Believe nothing, O monks, merely because you have been
told it . . . or because it is traditional, or because you
yourselves have imagined it. Do not believe what your
teacher tells you merely out of respect for the teacher. But
whatsoever, after due examination and analysis, you find to
be conducive to the good, the benefit, the welfare of all
beings—that doctrine believe and cling to, and take it as
your guide.*

- The Buddha

*We are under the influence of an illusion of permanence,
so we think there is always lots of time remaining. This
mistaken belief puts us in great danger of wasting our lives
in procrastination.*

- Dalai Lama

*The mouse eats cat food.
The cat bowl is broken.
What does this mean?*

- Zen Koan

When we are not sure, we are alive.

- Graham Greene

Who knows this morning what will happen tonight?

- Chinese Proverb

Let the learner direct his own learning.

- John Holt

In order to be irreplaceable, one must always be different.

- Coco Chanel

There is no solution, for there is no problem.

- Marcel Duchamp

If you want to accomplish something big, you'll have to do it bit by bit, one step at a time.

- Pam Cooper

There's still time, but there ain't forever.

- Rick Sylvester

We cannot put off living until we are ready. The most salient characteristic of life is its urgency, "here and now" without any postponement. Life is fired at us point blank.

- José Ortega y Gasset

113

Whatever gets you through the night.

- John Lennon

All this will not be finished in the first one hundred days. Nor will it be finished in the first one thousand days, nor in the life of this Administration, nor even perhaps in our lifetime on this planet. But let us begin.

- John F. Kennedy

In dreams begins responsibility.

- William Butler Yeats

The past is past. The future is now.

- David Voluck

Life is like poker. Part of it is knowing the odds. The rest is luck and a little magic.

- T.U. Snow

This time, like all times, is a very good one, if we but know what to do with it.

- Ralph Waldo Emerson

The unexamined life is not worth living.

- Socrates

The world is full of stories, and the stories are all one.

- Mitch Albom

There is the world as it is, and the world as it should be, and too often we accept the great divide between the two, rather than fight for, and live for, and believe that everyday we can move closer to the world as it should be.

- Jon Wunrow

Forever is composed of now.

- Emily Dickinson

The quest for certainty blocks the search for meaning. Uncertainty is the very condition to impel man to unfold his powers.

- Erich Fromm

Do not travel to other dusty lands, forsaking your own sitting place. If you cannot find the truth where you are now, you will never find it.

- Dogen

Few will have the greatness to bend history itself; but each of us can work to change a small portion of events, and on the total of all those acts will be written the history of this generation.

- Robert F. Kennedy

A permanent state of transition is man's most noble condition.

- Juan Ramon Jimenez

CAMARADERIE AND TEAMWORK

Very few climbers venture out to the mountains or cliffs alone. Other than the sport of bouldering, very few successful climbs are done solo. Viewed from afar, most extreme sports seem to be solo endeavors, but each has its own group of followers, and each involves, at some level, a dependence on others. Each of us, whether a climber, surfer, skier, biker, or diver, is part of a larger group of risk takers and fellow believers, and all to often our success depends on others.

People who adventure together share a special bond. They trust each other, encourage each other, and time after time put their life into each other's hands. Partners in risk see each other at their worst, at their most frustrated, at their most exhausted, at their most vulnerable, and at their most exhilarated. In a world where most people just can't grasp why we do what we do, the understanding and acceptance of the tribe of fellow risk-takers creates a safe haven.

I used to joke that I'd spent more nights sleeping next to my climbing partner Anthony over the years than I had spent sleeping next to my girlfriend (who is now my wife). In the mountains, camaraderie is defined by spending weeks at a time in a small tent barely big enough to fit two grown men amidst piles of jumbled gear, smelly socks, unwashed bodies, leaky pee bottles, and rancid flatulence, all the while laying in your sleeping bag dreaming about the next climb and when you might get to do it all over again.

Getting climbers and other adventurers to play together, to put their egos and aspirations aside for the good of the whole is difficult, and at times impossible. Casey Stengel, one of baseball's most famous managers, once said, "Getting good players is easy. Getting them to play together, that's the hard part." Most risky ventures (whether they be outdoor adventures, pursuing significant relationships, or parenting, etc.) are "team sports" and involve coming to some level of agreement on goals and the level of risk taking that everyone in the group is willing to accept. These are often difficult decisions when choosing a partner, and even more difficult once the adventure begins.

Sacrificing your chance at the summit for the good of the team is a tough pill to swallow. Being forced to end a trip because someone on the team got sick or injured can create resentment and ill feelings, even among the best of friends. Being willing to sacrifice and cooperate and communicate and tolerate and forego a long-held goal are essential to good teamwork and healthy relationships—and to a deeper sense of interpersonal connection, both during the endeavor and in every day life.

But none of these things are easy, and often they are accompanied by some level of pain or discomfort. Risk taking tests even the best relationships. So, why do the memories of most adventures revolve around the people we were with? Why is camaraderie a big part of why many risk takers continue to step back into the ring? And what

are some of the keys to a successful adventure partnership?
Read on for some of these answers.

Behind a temple was a vine with many squashes growing on it. One day a fight broke out among them, and the squashes split up into angry groups, making a big racket. Hearing the uproar, the head priest went outside, saw the quarrelling squash, and scolded them: "Hey! Squashes! Why are you fighting? Now, everybody do zazen."

The priest taught them how, showing them how to fold their legs and sit up straight, and as the squashes began to follow the priest's instructions, they calmed down and stopped fighting.

"Now," the priest said, "everyone put your hand on top of your head."

When the squashes felt the top of their heads, they found something attached there, which turned out to be the vine that connected them all together.

"What a mistake!" the squashes said, realizing their predicament, "We're actually all tied together, living just one life." From that moment on the squashes never again fought.

- Zen Story

Things derive their being and nature by mutual dependence and are nothing in themselves.

- Nagarjuna

Together we knew toil, joy and pain. My fervent wish is that the nine of us who were united in the face of death should remain fraternally united through life.

- Maurice Herzog

Question: "Bob, do you always enjoy swimming upstream?"
Bob: "No, occasionally I'd like some company."

- Bob Meadows

We must love each other
Because we share the earth's water,
We share the vegetation of the earth.
Under the same sun and moon,
We all wrinkle and grow old.
And we should love each other
Because we all cry while throwing time's stones
Into the rivers of the earth.
We tumble into the wind
Without knowing one another.
Like falling leaves or scuttling beetles,
We all separated and dispersed.

- Chung Hee Moon

Until you corner a skunk, you don't know lonesome.

- Hank Ketchum

Looking back on those wild, free days in the open I realize that my happiest memories are of the suntanned faces of my old companions.

- Belmore Browne

Speak to me heart
All things renew
Hearts will mend
Around the bend
Paths that cross
Will cross again.

> \- Lyrics of "Paths That Cross" by Patti Smith

Be kind, for everyone you meet is fighting a great battle.

> \- Philo of Alexandria

When you say, "I'm sorry," look the person in the eye.

> \- Unknown

Without friends no one would choose to live, though he had all other goods.

> \- Aristotle

The ideal criteria (for an expedition partner) is level-headedness, patience, and above all, good nature towards fellow human beings.

> \- Ranulph Fiennes

Count no day lost in which you waited your turn, took only your share, and sought advantage over no one.

> \- Robert Brault

Twice in my life I have experienced deep depression. Both times various friends tried to rescue me with well-intended encouragement and advice. . . . In the midst of my depression I had a friend who took a different tack. Every afternoon at around four o'clock he came to me, sat me in a chair, removed my shoes, and massaged my feet. He hardly said a word, but he was there, he was with me. He was a lifeline for me. He had no need to fix me. He knew the meaning of compassion.

- Parker J. Palmer

Every morning, our first thought should be a wish to devote the day to the good of all living beings.

- Dilgo Khyentse Rinpoche

When men climb on a great mountain together, the rope between them is more than a mere physical aid to the ascent; it is a symbol of the spirit of the enterprise. It is a symbol of men banded together in a common effort of will and strength against their only true enemies: inertia, cowardice, greed, ignorance, and all weaknesses of the spirit.

- Charles Houston

Nirvana may be the final object of attainment, but at the moment, it is difficult to reach. Thus, the practical and realistic aim is compassion, a warm heart, serving other people, helping others, respecting others, being less selfish.

- Dalai Lama

The least slip on the part of my companion and I should be dead . . . yet I was more worried about my own possible clumsiness than his.

- Lionel Terray

Ants, to cite just one example, work unselfishly for the community; we humans sometimes do not look good by comparison.

- Dalai Lama

If there is a deeper and most lasting message behind our venture than the mere passing sensation of a physical feat, I believe this to be the value of comradeship and the many virtues which combine to create it. Comradeship, regardless of race or creed, is forged among high mountains, through the difficulties and dangers to which they expose those who aspire to climb them, the need to combine the efforts to attain their goal, the thrills of an adventure shared together.

- Sir John Hunt

Wise people serve others sincerely, putting the needs of others above their own.

- Dalai Lama

If collaboration is transformation, can we agree to work together to turn the world upside down?

- Jon Wunrow

Evolve a joint craziness with someone you are safe with.

- Carl Whitaker

There are two levels of spirituality. One involves religious faith. The other involves being a happy, compassionate and good person. If you choose only one, choose the later.

- Dalai Lama

Piglet sidled up to Pooh from behind.
"Pooh?" he whispered.
"Yes, Piglet?"
"Nothing," said Piglet, taking Pooh's paw. "I just wanted to be sure of you."

- Excerpt from *The House at Pooh Corner* by A.A. Milne

Remember that the best relationship is one in which your love for each other exceeds your need for each other.

- Dalai Lama

Only keep the question: "What is the best way of helping other people?"

- Seung Sahn

If we each selfishly pursue only what we believe to be in our own interest, without caring about the needs of others, we not only may end up harming others but also ourselves.

- Dalai Lama

HARDSHIP AND WHAT
IT CAN TEACH US

Life isn't always easy or fair. Life can often be hard, confusing, and depressing. We all experience unforeseen circumstances, use poor judgment, receive our fair share of karma, and have to deal with the actions of others or our own inaction. Shit happens. And if it hasn't for a while, it will. This isn't a fatalistic view of life. Experiencing hard times is just part of the human condition, part of being alive. Hardships will come, and how we deal with them not only can impact the ultimate outcome, but can teach us a lot about ourselves.

How do you respond when things aren't going your way? Are you better at solving other people's problems than you are at solving your own? What do you choose to do when your life takes an unplanned U-turn in a direction you don't want to be heading? U.S. Congresswoman Gabby Giffords, one year after being shot in the head in a grocery

127

store parking lot while meeting with her constituents, asked, "What do you do when the life you are given is not the life you expected?" Do you hide or go into a state of denial? Do you blame the situation on someone else? Do you temporarily self-medicate the problem away? Do you just keep running faster and faster and stay as busy and distracted as possible, keeping the problem in your rear view mirror?

The challenges and hardships that adventurers and risk takers experience take the form of physical pain, fear, exhaustion, high altitude, illness and injury, broken bones and broken spirits, loneliness, extreme weather, waning confidence, objective challenges that exceed our ability, and more. The challenges and hardships that we face in everyday life aren't that much different. At one point or another in all of our lives we will be forced to face illness and injury, a loss of confidence, loneliness, fear, or a challenge that definitely seems like more than we can handle. The knowledge that we are not alone in our suffering, that there are others that have faced similar hardships and survived, can bring some amount of hope and eventually peace. Suffering and hardship is part of our human condition. It's one thing that we all share. Experiencing hardships can bring people together, as the writer C.S. Lewis once observed, "Suffering drives us from our misery, and into the world of others."

When you are going through difficulties in your personal life, or on the trail, do you escape any way that your can, or do you do what Winston Churchill advised when he said, "If you are going through hell, keep going"? In my humble estimation, surviving life's hardships, and coming out on the other side in good or better shape has everything to do with our attitude. I remember reading somewhere that only ten percent of living through a survival situation depends on the equipment you have and the knowledge of how to properly use it. The other ninety percent of survival depends on mental attitude. The belief you will survive, the drive to survive, the determination to not accept death or defeat as an option, and the commitment to take just one more breath, and then one more after that, can make all the difference, especially when taking another breath or dying are your only options.

Hardships can be our best teachers if we are open to what we are being taught, and not just obsessed with how bad things are. Sometimes we are only able to glimpse what it is we are supposed to learn when we are in the depths of our despair. There is something about being at the bottom of a pit in life, stripped of our defenses, or staring death in the eye at altitude on a mountain, that can allow us to see our way out. Ralph Waldo Emerson once wrote, "When it is dark enough, you can see the stars." But to see the stars in the midst of the darkness, we have to look up. When we "look up" and move away from blame, hopelessness, and fatalistic thinking, and we carefully examine how we got into the situation we are in and what we can do about it, we begin to see the stars on the darkest of nights.

As a climber, I've learned time and again that if I can muster the courage, self-confidence, endurance, and clear thinking that I need to survive and succeed in the mountains and live solely in the moment, then I not only have a chance of reaching the summit, but I'll also be able to face and handle anything once I get home. Hardships in life, and in the mountains, can only teach us something if we are open to learning. The quotes in this section offer a glimpse of the stars that are out there, even in the darkest of nights.

If you fell down yesterday, stand up today.

> - H.G.Wells

From the bottom, I see the climb up!

> - Paula Peterson

Every strike brings me closer to the next home run.

> - Babe Ruth

I might be a slow walker, but I refuse to stop walking.

> - Jon Wunrow

A hero is no braver than an ordinary man, but he is brave five minutes longer.

> - Ralph Waldo Emerson

Don't fight forces, use them.

> - R. Buckminster Fuller

It is under the greatest adversity that there exists the greatest potential for doing good, both for oneself and others.

> - Dalai Lama

Autobiography in Five Short Chapters

Ch. I: I walk down the street. There is a deep hole in the sidewalk. I fall in. I am lost . . . I am helpless. It isn't my fault. It takes forever to find a way out.

Ch. II: I walk down the same street. There is a deep hole in the sidewalk. I pretend I don't see it. I fall in again. I can't believe I am in the same place. But, it isn't my fault. It still takes a long time to get out.

Ch. III: I walk down the same street. There is a deep hole in the sidewalk. I see it is there. I still fall in . . . it's a habit. My eyes are open. I know where I am. It is my fault. I get out immediately.

Ch. IV: I walk down the same street. There is a deep hole in the sidewalk. I walk around it.

Ch. V: I walk down a different street.

- Portia Nelson

No problem is too big, as long as you have a big enough plastic bag.

- Unknown

No one is a winner the day before the race.

- Ben Taylor

Pain is only weakness leaving the body.

- Tom Muccia

We do not receive wisdom, we must discover it for ourselves, after a journey through the wilderness, which no one else can make for us.

- Marcel Proust

To have a great adventure, and to survive, requires good judgment. Good judgment comes from experience. Experience, of course, is the result of poor judgment.

- Geoff Tabin

Have no fear of perfection. You'll never reach it.

- Salvador Dali

Live in the world relying on the self alone as a foundation, be freed from all things, depending on no thing.

- The Dhammapada

Indeed whatever agonies and miseries the sufferer may endure on his pilgrimage to the heights, and however often he may swear never to return there, longing to do so is certain to recur.

- C.F. Meade

Since the house is on fire, let us warm ourselves.

- Italian Proverb

People may not get all that they work for. But they certainly must work for all that they get.

- Frederick Douglass

Although the climb was rarely pleasurable, it was nevertheless unforgettable.

- Ian McNaught-Davis

There is no coming to consciousness without pain.

- Car Gustav Jung

That's one of the remarkable things about life. It's never so bad that it can't get worse.

- Bill Watterson

To be human, you must bear witness to justice. Justice is what love looks like in public—to be human is to love and be loved.

- Cornell West

There is absolutely no hope of beating the weeds, which are out there growing back this very moment. I need to reframe this task so that my thinking fits reality and sends me outside with the proper attitude. When I step out on the patio, I'm not fighting the weeds. I'm joining them.

- Linda Witner

Undergoing small sufferings in this lifetime can purify the karma of many ill deeds accumulated in former lifetimes.

- Dalai Lama

Pissing through six inches of clothes with a three-inch penis!

- Anonymous Everest summiteer
when asked what was the hardest thing
about climbing Mt.Everest

Tragic circumstances help you develop inner strength, the courage to face them without emotional breakdown. Who teaches this? Not your friend, but your enemy.

- Dalai Lama

As I hammered in the last bolt and staggered over the rim, it was not at all clear to me who was the conqueror and who was the conquered. I do recall that El Cap seemed to be in much better condition than I was.

- Warren Harding

One person may feel demoralized and become sort of paralyzed, thinking, There is no hope, I lost my job, what am I supposed to do? But another individual in the same situation might look at it as an opportunity to make some changes. As a challenge. So that is the more positive way, the more proactive way of dealing with this problem. But of course it is not easy.

- Dalai Lama

I'd rather wear out then rust out.

- Dick Bass

It's better to burn out than it is to rust.

- Neil Young

The world is so constructed, that if you wish to enjoy its pleasures, you also must endure its pains.

- Swami Brahmananda

Adversity introduces man to himself.

- Albert Einstein

So let us go forward, quietly, each on his own path, forever making for the light.

- Vincent Van Gogh

The best way out is always through.

- Robert Frost

The race is not always to the swift, but to those who keep on running.

- Unknown

Something of our personality has gone into every mountain on which we have spent our strength and on which our thoughts have rested, and something of its personality has come into ours and had its small effect on everything that has come within our influence.

- R. L. G. Irving

I seemed to discover the deep significance of existence of which till then I had been unaware. I saw that it was better to be true than to be strong.

- Maurice Herzog

Letting Go. The mountain of release is such that the ascent is most painful at the start, below. The more you rise, the milder it will be. And when the slope feels gentle to the point that climbing up sheer rock is effortless, as though you were gliding downstream in a boat, then you will have arrived where this path ends.

- Dante

The torch of doubt and chaos, this is what the sage steers by.

- Chuang-Tzu

When worn out and seeking an inn—
Wisteria flowers!

- Basho

Mexico City, 1968 – Out of the cold darkness he came. John Stephen Akhwari, of Tanzania, entered at the far end of the stadium, pain hobbling his every step, his leg bloody and bandaged. The winner of the Olympic marathon had been declared over an hour earlier. Only a few spectators remained. But the lone runner pressed on. As he crossed the finish line, the small crowd roared out its appreciation. Afterward, a reporter asked the runner why he had not retired from the race, since he had no chance of winning. He seemed confused by the question. Finally, he answered, "My country did not send me to Mexico City to start the race. They sent me to finish."

- Excerpt from *Amazing but True Sports Stories* by Steve Riach

Even in the driest hole one can sometimes find water.

- Zen Saying

Sometimes life's lessons may not be those you would have chosen to learn.

- Unknown

Sometimes when feeling lost it is best to continue on uphill into the driving wind and hail because the summit is the only vantage point for finding the trail to our intended destination, wherever that is.

- Stormy Hamar

When we pass through difficulties, there is no room to pretend.

- Dalai Lama

Did you not know that at the edge of a deep valley there is an excellent pine tree,
Growing up straight in spite of the many years of cold?

- Keizan Zenji

By your stumbling,
The world is perfected.

- Sri Aurobindo

A Zen master's life is one continuous mistake.

- Dogen

Pain is inevitable. Misery is optional.

- Hyrum W. Smith

When you do something, you should burn yourself completely, like a good bonfire, leaving no trace of yourself.

- Shunryu Suzuki

If you focus too closely, too intensely, on a problem when it occurs, it appears uncontrollable. But if you compare that event with some other greater event, look at the same problem from a distance, then it appears smaller and less overwhelming.

- Dalai Lama

Everything we do is futile, but we must do it anyway.

- Mahatma Gandhi

If someone prays for patience, does God give them patience, or the opportunity to be patient? If someone prays for courage, does God give them courage, or the opportunity to be courageous?

- *Evan Almighty*, Film, 2007

Strategy is important, but it's execution that counts.

- Unknown

Challenge doesn't build character, it reveals it.

- Unknown

When a dog is chasing after you, whistle for him.

- Ralph Waldo Emerson

No more prizes for predicting rain. Prizes only for building arks.

- Louis V. Gerstner, Jr.

Beyond 40 degrees south, there is no law.
Beyond 50 degrees south, there is no God.

- 19th Century Whaler's Saying

The heart that breaks open can contain the whole universe.

-Joanna Macy

We master our minutes, or become slaves to them;
We use them, or they use us.

- William A. Ward

The difference between a successful person and others is not a lack of strength, not a lack of knowledge, but rather a lack of will.

- Vince Lombardi

Most of the important things in the world have been accomplished by people who have kept on trying when there seemed to be no hope at all.

- Dale Carnegie

Success is a little like wrestling a gorilla. You don't quit when you're tired. You quit when the gorilla is tired.

- Robert Strauss

Life, Stormy says, is not about how fast you run or even with what degree of grace. It's about perseverance, about staying on your feet and slogging forward no matter what.

- Dean Koontz

If you don't let go, you can't fall off.

- Jerry Moffat

Once you learn to quit, it becomes a habit.

- Vince Lombardi

I think this is when most people give up on their stories. They come out of college wanting to change the world, wanting to get married, wanting to have kids and change the way people buy office supplies. But they get into the middle and discover it was harder than they thought. They can't see the distant shore anymore, and they wonder if their paddling is moving them forward. None of the trees behind them are getting smaller and none of the trees ahead are getting bigger. They take it out on their spouses, and they go looking for an easier story.

- Donald Miller

I can accept failure. Everybody fails at something. But I can not accept not trying.

- Michael Jordan

TAKING RISKS

Why do people take risks? Or, one could ask, why don't people take risks? We all know both kinds of people: those who take risks in life—in love, at work, at play—and those who don't seem to take any risks at all, those who just play it safe, who live in a bubble of security and predictability.

We all live our lives and make daily decisions that fall somewhere on the risk-taking continuum. Getting in the car and going for a drive on a busy street is making a decision that accepts a certain level of risk. Having unprotected sex, maintaining an unhealthy diet, sitting on the couch and watching TV five hours a day, remaining in a high stress job or relationship, or riding a roller coaster are all decisions and behaviors that involve a degree of risk. We take risks every day. What I've always found a bit odd is that most people think nothing of driving seventy or eighty miles per hour down a busy highway, sometimes without wearing a seatbelt, with other speeding cars. These people think nothing of the fact that at these speeds, any number of dangerous things could happen. This same person may never consider tying into the end of a rope that is safely anchored with multiple back-ups, and repel down a rock face. I have friends who would never consider traveling through a jungle for fear of snakes and spiders, but think nothing of having a few drinks and then driving home, or don't give a second thought to working in a high stress job that is more likely to kill them.

Not only do we all live our lives somewhere on the risk continuum, our logical assessment of the danger we face on a regular basis is somehow skewed or misinformed, and almost entirely subjectively based on our individual perceptions. Something that seems very risky to you may not feel like a risk at all to me. That, in part, is a matter of perception. In other situations, one may not be aware of the level of risk because we simply don't have enough information. We can often be ignorant to how dangerous a situation really is, and don't know that a particular behavior is unsafe. In other cases, our previous experience or familiarity in doing something can actually reduce the inherent risk in an activity or at least reduce our perception that something is risky or dangerous. So the assessment we each make of what is and is not a risky behavior is based on individual perceptions, experience, and a knowledge base.

The biggest obstacle that prevents most of us from taking risks in life is, quite simply, fear. We are afraid that the result of taking a risk will be failure or some equally uncomfortable feeling or circumstance. For example, the fear of loneliness or heartbreak may prevent us from becoming involved in a new relationship. We are afraid that if we take a risk, we might get hurt or worse, we might die. We are afraid that we might fail or be humiliated and because of these fears, we often decide to play it safe. The fear of loss, rejection, loneliness, injury, or death wins out over the potential of happiness, contentment, seeing and learning new things, accomplishment, increased self-confidence, or even financial gain that could come from taking the risk. So, one of the keys to taking more risks in life is learning how to manage our fears.

Most adventurers are risk takers. To better understand why they risk, re-read the chapter in this book titled "Why Play a Risky Game?" The quotes below outline some of the reasons why it might be worth increasing your level of risk-taking and why stepping out of your safety zone could be a good decision. Being courageous and taking risks does not mean that your fear has disappeared. Being courageous is moving forward into the unknown, while still being afraid, with the belief that something amazing awaits you on the other side.

One more thought about risk taking: whether it is adrenaline, or dopamine or something else, "life on the wire," as the great Karl Wallenda called it, can become addictive. The physical and emotional rush that comes with taking a risk and coming out on the other side relatively unscathed can push some of us to want to recreate that same feeling again and again. Life off the wire can seem somehow diminished, less in focus, less fulfilling, and even depressing. Consequently some of us spend a lot of our time planning and preparing for our next walk on the high wire. Friedrich Nietzsche is no intellectual slouch, and even he understood life on the wire when he said, "the secret of knowing the most fertile experiences and the greatest joys in life, is to live dangerously."

Risk implies an unknowable element that may result in tragedy. Yet a greater human tragedy is never to venture beyond the known.

- Rhea Dodd

All of us have the potential to pull off some pretty incredible things. The difference is most people are too afraid of taking the first step.

- Jon Wunrow

Only those who risk going too far can possibly find out how far it is possible to go.

- T.S. Eliot

The world needs risk takers. They inspire, challenge, and encourage. They set off sparks, igniting fires that burn long after their passing. They dare the impossible, but not without cost.

- Maria Coffey

Fear is an illusion.

- Michael Jordan

Leap and the net will appear.

- John Burroughs

146

But he'd learned long ago that a life lived without risks pretty much wasn't worth living. Life rewarded courage, even when that first step was taken neck-deep in fear.

- Excerpt from *Within My Heart* by Tamara Alexander

What great thing would you attempt if you knew you could not fail?

- Robert Schuller

You do the thing you're scared shitless of and then you get your courage. Not before. That's the way it works.

- *Three Kings*, Film, 1999

Necessity is the mother of taking chances.

- Mark Twain

Progress always involves risks. You can't steal second base and keep your foot on first.

- Frederick Wilcox

I'm not fearless. I often feel afraid. I just try not to let fear stop me.

- Jon Wunrow

Go out on a limb, because that is where the fruit is.

- Jimmy Carter

If you are a brave man, you will do nothing. If you are fearful you may do much, for none but cowards have need to prove their bravery.

- Apsley Cherry-Garrard

It is not because things are difficult that we dare not venture. It's because we dare not venture that they are difficult.

- Seneca

Life is being on the wire. Everything else is just waiting.

- Karl Wallenda

If things seem under control, you're just not going fast enough.

- Mario Andretti

We have to remember that if we are talking about true risk, occasionally there has to be a price paid.

- Royal Robbins

Do not fear mistakes. There are none.

- Miles Davis

Nothing will be attempted, if all possible objections must be first overcome.

- Samuel Johnson

I'm afraid to be afraid.

- Catherine Destivelle

You'll always miss 100 percent of the shots you don't take.

- Wayne Gretzky

People who don't take risks generally make about two big mistakes a year. People who do take risks make about two big mistakes a year.

- Peter Drucker

Let me not pray to be sheltered from dangers, but to be fearless in facing them. Let me not beg for the stilling of my pain, but for the heart to conquer it.

- Rabindranath Tagore

"What's the bravest thing you ever did?"
He spat on the road a bloody phlegm. "Getting up this
morning," he said.

- Excerpt from *The Road* by Cormac McCarthy

I told him my concern about avalanche danger on the
route, but Peter was full of confidence. He had watched the
face on many occasions, he told me, and had never seen an
avalanche sweep down. I argued no longer. I too had never
actually seen an avalanche falling down the face, although
they must come down sometimes, I felt, judging from the
debris at the bottom. I don't think there is anything very
clever about killing yourself off, or even about having a fall
and surviving.

- Sir Edmund Hillary on advising his son Peter on
their intended ascent of the west face of Ama Dablam

Dear Lord, please don't let me fuck up.

- Attributed to Alan Shepard

I don't want to die without any scars.

- Excerpt from *Fight Club*
by Chuck Palahniuk

All serious daring starts from within.

- Eudora Welty

Eliminate something superfluous from your life. Break a habit. Do something that makes you feel insecure. Carry out an action with complete attention and intensity, as if it were your last.

- Piero Ferrucci

Mountains are not fair or unfair—they are just dangerous.

- Reinhold Messner

The devotion of the greatest is to encounter risk and danger, and play dice for death.

- Friedrich Nietzsche

We took risks. We knew we took them. Things have come out against us. We have no cause for complaint.

- Found in Robert F. Scott's diary after he and his party froze to death in Antarctica

To put yourself into a situation where a mistake cannot necessarily be recouped, where the life you lose may be your own, clears the head wonderfully. It puts domestic problems into proportion and adds an element of seriousness to your drab, routine life.

- A. Alvarez

Deep within us I think we know that we need challenge and danger, and the risk and hurt that will sometimes follow. "Dangerous" sports would not be as popular as they are if this were not so. Mountain climbing is not the only way of dealing with an over-organized, over-protective society. But it is one good way.

- Woodrow Wilson Sayre

In order to climb properly on a big peak one must free oneself of fear. This means you must write yourself off before any big climb. You must say to yourself, "I may die here."

- Doug Scott

Walking along the edge of a sword,
Running over jagged ice;
You need take no steps—
Let go your hold on the cliff!

- Philip Kapleau

Endurance, fear, suffering, cold, and the state between survival and death are such strong experiences that we want them again and again. We become addicted. Strangely, we strive to come back safely; and being back, we seek to return, once more, to danger.

- Reinhold Messner

The reason it was so scary was that there was only one climber capable of rescuing us, and that was Layton Kor, and he was in Colorado.

- Yvon Chouinard

Concerning all acts of initiative (and creation), there is one elementary truth, the ignorance of which kills countless ideas and splendid plans: that the moment one definitely commits oneself, then providence moves too. A whole stream of events issue from the decision, raising in one's favor all manner of unforeseen incidents, meetings and material assistance, which no man could have dreamt would have come his way.

- W.H. Murray

Dream big and dare to fail. Young and old. Dream big and dare to fail.

- Norman Vaughn

We promise according to our hopes, and perform according to our fears.

- Francios de La Rochefoucauld

Do one thing every day that scares you.

- Eleanor Roosevelt

It is to conquer fear that one becomes a climber. The climber experiences life to its extreme. A climber is not crazy. He is not out to get himself killed. He knows what life is worth. He is in love with living.

- Walter Bonatti

Play for more than you can afford to lose, then you will learn the game.

- Winston Churchill

We commenced plugging up in foot-deep steps with a thin wind crust on top of precious little belay for the ice-axe. It was altogether most unsatisfactory and whenever I felt feelings of fear regarding it, I'd say to myself, "Forget it!" This is Everest and you've got to take a few risks.

- Sir Edmund Hillary

Q: What's cold and black and lies at the bottom of the wastebasket?
A: A Himalayan climber's toes.

- Unknown

Fear of the unknown is the greatest fear of all, but we just went for it.

- Yvon Chouinard

I feel safe in the mountains because nothing heinous is going to happen to me. The risk to climbing is nothing compared to always worrying if someone is going to abduct you and kill you. My worst fear is ending up locked in a basement by some evil person. Wouldn't you rather get hit by a rock on the side of a mountain than have that happen?

- Steph Davies

The pleasure of risk is in the control needed to ride it with assurance so that what appears dangerous to the outsider is, to the participant, simply a matter of intelligence, skill, intuition, coordination—in a word, experience. Climbing in particular, is a paradoxically intellectual pastime, but with this difference: you have to think with your body. Every move has to be worked out in terms of playing chess with your body. If I make a mistake the consequences are immediate, obvious, embarrassing, and possibly painful. For a brief period I am directly responsible for my actions. In that beautiful, silent world of mountains, it seems to me worth a little risk.

- A. Alvarez

It's not like mountaineering, because it's so immediate. It scares the shit out of you when it goes wrong. You suddenly get a sense of this huge elemental power and you go, "What the fuck are we doing . . . this is stupid." And then you get out of it alive and you go, "Well that wasn't too bad, was it?" You start using the same rationale as when you're climbing.

- Joe Simpson, talking of paragliding

Fear is one of the countless sensations felt by the climber and which, combined with others, gives him the reason for his existence. Beware if you do not experience fear in the mountains. Not to do so would mean that one was devoid of feeling and no longer able to experience the supreme joy of knowing that one has mastered fear. Mountaineering can indeed be more dangerous than any other human activity, but if one comes to the mountains carefully prepared and observes reasonable prudence, it becomes something far different from mere foolish recklessness.

- Walter Bonatti

A ship is always safe at the shore—but that is not what it is built for.

- Albert Einstein

Habit, laziness, and fear conspire to keep us comfortable within the familiar.

- Jane Hirshfield

A mistake proves that someone stopped talking long enough to do something.

- Phoenix Flame

Decision making is risk taking.

- Tom Clarke

The wind only, I am afraid of.

> \- Chippewa Song

Security is mostly a superstition. It doesn't exist in nature, nor do the children of men experience it. Avoiding danger is no safer in the long run than outright exposure. Life is either a daring adventure, or nothing.

> \- Helen Keller

Remember that great love and great achievements involve great risk.

> \- Dalai Lama

When you are hanging by your hands from a mountain ledge and can let go, not thinking of life or death, then you will have true freedom. You can see the wooden dog eating steel and shitting fire. You can shake hands with the hairy-shelled turtle and rabbit with horns. You can learn to play the flute that has no holes. But where does the sound of the flute come from?

> \- Seung Sahn

If you don't fail, then perhaps you aren't taking enough risks.

> \- Unknown

Failure is not a crime. Low aim is.

- John Wooden, former UCLA basketball coach

He that fears not, gives advantage to the danger.

- Francis Quarles

You cannot discover new oceans unless you have the courage to lose sight of the shore.

- Andre Gide

Here, in my security, I've put a limit on my potential and possibility.

- Unknown

What about those who drive in rush hour traffic or work a hundred hours a week? For experienced mountaineers, the odds of survival, if we look at the data carefully, are definitely better than for many other endeavors, especially if we meet the challenges with skill and experience.

-Jed Williamson

Each climber loses one finger or one toe once in a while. This is a small but important reason for Polish climbers' success. Western climbers have not lost as many fingers or toes.

- Wanda Rutkiewicz

Fear and dread are my life insurance.

- Erhard Loretan

It is the momentary carelessness in easy places, the lapsed attention, or the wandering look that is the usual parent of disaster.

- Albert F. Mummery

And today I know that the path between tomb and towering heights is extremely narrow.

- Reinhold Messner

There are old climbers, and there are bold climbers, but there are no old bold climbers.

- Unknown

We're not going to be famous, unless we get down alive.

- Ed Webster, descending Everest's Kangshung Face after summiting without oxygen

The moment of terror is the beginning of life, Mike, so take the "No Fear" stickers off your truck.

- Marc Twight

Now I don't worry about falling, but I'm no different than any of those women: I'm not bold, I'm not brave; in fact, I'm a total chicken-shit.

- Shelley Presson

A good scare is worth more to a man than good advice.

- Ed Howe

I want to be one of those people who, if he fails, fails greatly because of his extreme efforts.

- Paraphrased from Theodore Roosevelt

Reaching for the possible is not worth the effort.

- Wlodzimierz Pietrzak

It takes a lot of courage to release the familiar and seemingly secure, to embrace the new. But there is no real security in what is no longer meaningful. There is more security in the adventurous and exciting, for in movement there is life, and in change there is power.

- Alan Cohen

Break through the impassable barrier and get to know the opening beyond.

- Fo-hsing T'ai

160

Pieces are coming off my bad ear.

> - John Edwards, during his 1967
> winter climb of Denali

It's not an adventure until something goes wrong.

> - Yvon Chouinard

DEATH

To risk death while protecting a loved one or protecting one's country; or to stand in the face of injustice and risk death for a greater good, like thousands did in Tiananmen Square or the Arab Spring; to risk death for reasons like these, makes some sort of sense to most of us. Moral sense. Practical sense. Dying in the process of contributing to a greater good. But to risk death in the pursuit of an extreme adventure or sport? To many people, that makes no sense. It is sense-less. It's crazy. It's selfish. So why do some choose to push the limits of climbing or skiing or surfing or BASE jumping right to the edge? To the edge of death.

The previous chapter on "Taking Risks" explores the idea that the pursuits of most climbers are no more dangerous than the acceptable behaviors of others in everyday life, and that all of our behaviors lie somewhere on the risk continuum. We've been acculturated to believe that climbing or paragliding or skydiving or spelunking are more dangerous than driving to work or taking a commercial flight across the country, but maybe that just isn't so.

In a lot of ways, death and a fear of dying is a matter of perspective. This perspective is influenced by our opinions and beliefs about the reasons we are on this earth, and what, if anything, comes after death. However, whether we choose to fear death or embrace it, to deny it or accept it, we all have one thing in common: at some point we will all die. Once we acknowledge that we are all going to die and that it's just a matter of when, we begin to understand that dying is one experience that we will all share and need not fear. We are born, we feel love and sadness, our heart beats and our lungs fill with air, and we die. These are normal and universal notes in the rhythms of life.

To me, the issue isn't when or how I'm going to die, it's how I am choosing to live in the moments that I have. How do I choose to act and think and treat others in this moment, right now, and then in the next? Most of us live in the fantasy that we all have plenty of time, that we have all the time in the world. Author and Buddhist teacher Jack Kornfield reminds us, "The trouble is that you think you have time." Thinking that we have all the time in the world, and that we will live to a ripe old age, gives us the permission to put things off. This is the dilemma that Kornfield is referring to. We delay. We make excuses. We put off saying "I'm sorry" until tomorrow; we wait to try something new or take a risk until the time is right; we don't take that trip we've always dreamed of, until after we retire. And then life or death intervenes, and tomorrow never comes. People on their deathbeds have a way of seeing their lives more clearly. Why is that? What is it about facing death that brings life and priorities into focus? How can we maintain this "death perspective" every minute of every day? What do you need to do to change your perspective so that you live every day as if it were your last?

Another belief about life and death that can cause us a lot of pain is the belief that we deserve a long life. People talk of feeling cheated when a young person dies, or a friend dies of a heart attack just before they reach retirement age, or a soldier dies before he had a chance to became a man. Life gives us no guarantees of longevity. None of the great books of religion or philosophy promise us a long life. We are given this moment and that's all we know for sure. Maybe the next moment will come and maybe it won't. Knowing this, how do we choose to live in this moment? Those of us who chose to engage in extreme sports seem to understand these things better than most, probably because more than once, we've been forced to face the inevitability of death directly and in the moment.

For whatever reasons, the following quotes about death are some of my favorites of the thousands of quotes I've collected. Read them carefully. Let them sink it. Living a full and meaningful life depends on a clear understanding of death.

Dying is not what scares me. What scares me is dying and not having made a difference.

- Miles Levin, who
died of cancer as a teenager

Living with the immediacy of death helps you sort out your priorities in life. It helps you to live a less trivial life.

- Sogyal Rinpoche

It makes you live the best life you can, when you realize that tomorrow isn't guaranteed, isn't assured, isn't real.

- Jon Wunrow

Summit or death, either way, I win.

- Rob Slater

The defining thing about climbing is that it kills you.

- Joe Simpson

To the well-organized mind, death is but the next great adventure.

- J.K. Rowling

The fear of death follows from a fear of life.

> \- Mark Twain

If we knew that tonight we were going to go blind, we would take a longing, last real look at every blade of grass, every cloud formation, every speck of dust, every rainbow— everything.

> \- Pema Chodron

It is true, I am afraid of dying. I am afraid of the world moving forward without me, of my absence going unnoticed. Is it selfish? Am I such a bad person for dreaming of a world that ends when I do? I don't mean the world ending with respect to me, but every set of eyes closing with mine.

> \- Jonathan Safran Foer

It's better to die laughing than to live each moment in fear.

> \- Michael Crichton

You see, we are all dying. It's only a matter of time. Some of us just die sooner than others.

> \- Dudjam Rinpoche

I hope I die before I get old.

> \- The Who

As my own life began to slip away, I was struck with an overwhelming sense of how wonderful it is to be alive.

- Art Davidson

If you're ever killed mountain climbing, then all that you've worked for is gone.

- Jim Whittaker

The world is fleeting; all things pass away. Or is it that we pass away and they stay?

- Lucian

In this short span between my fingertips and the smooth edge and these tense feet cramped to a crystal ledge, I hold the life of a man.

- Geoffrey Winthrop Young

If you fall, you die.

- Anonymous Climber

Men's resources of energy in the face of death are inexhaustible. When the end seems imminent, there still remain reserves, though it needs tremendous willpower to call them up.

- Maurice Herzog

I'm not afraid of death; I just don't want to be there when it happens.

- Woody Allen

Life is a candle before the wind.

- Japanese Poverb

The moment of death is impossible to predict. Who can say? Perhaps we will die tonight.

- Shabkar

To those men who are born for mountains the struggle can never end, until their lives end—to them it holds the very quintessence of living. . . .

- Elizabeth Knowlton

I do not fear death. I had been dead for billions and billions of years before I was born, and had not suffered the slightest inconvenience from it.

- Mark Twain

If you can't die doing it, it's not a sport, it's a game.

- Skydiving T-shirt

People living deeply have no fear of death.

- Anais Nin

Learn to hold loosely all that is not eternal.

- A. Maude Royden

I used to believe in reincarnation, but that was in a past life.

- Paul Krassner

I beg to urge you, everyone:
Life and death is a grave matter,
All things pass quickly away;
Each of you must be completely alert:
Never neglectful, never indulgent.

- Evening Message at Sesshin

This life of ours would not cause you sorrow
If you thought of it as like the mountain cherry blossoms
Which bloom and fade in a day.

- Murasaki Shikibu

No one here gets out alive.

- Jim Morrison

*Many people die at twenty-five and aren't buried until they
are seventy-five.*

- Ben Franklin

I want to see if I'm afraid to die.

- Layton Kor, before attempting a winter
ascent of Yosemite's Steck-Salathe Wall

*I'm the one that's got to die when it's time for me to die; so
let me live my life the way I want to.*

- Jimi Hendrix

*Dying cricket,
His song so full of life.*

- Basho

*They had seen so much of death that life mattered less than
the moments of being alive.*

- Excerpt from *Into the Silence:
The Great War, Mallory, and the
Conquest of Everest* by Wade Davis

*But for those men who are born for the mountains, the
struggle can never end until their lives end.*

- Warren Harding

Death is no more than passing from one room into another. But there's a difference for me, you know. Because in that other room I shall be able to see.

- Helen Keller

No one really knows why they are alive until they know what they'd die for.

- Martin Luther King, Jr.

For what is it to die, but to stand in the sun and melt into the wind? And when the Earth has claimed our limbs, then we shall truly dance.

- Khalil Gibran

Life is short. Tomorrow isn't guaranteed. It's crazy how many people live life like it's going to go on forever.

- Eric Scully

Let me respectfully remind you, life and death are of supreme importance.
Time swiftly passes by and opportunity is lost.
Each of us should strive to awaken.
Awaken! Take heed, do not squander your life.

- The Evening Gatha

The only preparation I can make for death is by fulfilling my present duties. This is the everlasting life.

> \- Ralph Waldo Emerson

Life is not a journey to the grave with the intention of arriving safely in a pretty and well-preserved body, but rather to skid in sideways, thoroughly used up, totally worn out, champagne in one hand . . . strawberries in the other and screaming: "Woo hoo! What a ride!"

> \- Hunter S. Thompson

Remember not to have a fatal accident, because the community will think climbing is a dangerous thing, your friends will be bummed . . . and you'll be dead.

> \- Kitty Calhoun

Death never takes the wise man by surprise, he is always ready to go.

> \- La Fontaine

Would that life were like the shadow cast by a wall or a tree, but it is like the shadow of a bird in flight.

> \- The Talmud

Do every act of your life as if it were your last.

> \- Marcus Aurelius

We cannot fully understand the beginning of something until we understand the end.

- George Spencer-Brown

He would not have wanted to die doing what he loved, but instead was not afraid to live without the buzz kill of being afraid of dying. When we are on the edge, we are finally consumed with nothing but the physical, spiritual, and mental nirvana that makes us whole.

- Written in honor of Lathrop Strang,
who died at age 46 while skiing the
Laundry Chute on Mount Sopris

If I had to live my life over again I should form the habit of nightly composing myself to thoughts of death. I would practice, as it were, the remembrance of death. There is no other practice which so intensifies life. Death, when it approaches, ought not to take one by surprise. It should be part of the full expectancy of life. Without an ever-present sense of death, life is insipid. You might as well live on the whites of eggs.

- Muriel Spark

I want death to find me planting cabbages, but caring little for it, and much more for my imperfect garden.

- Michel de Montaigne

Death, the most dreaded of evils, is therefore of no concern to us; For while we exist death is not present, and when death is present we no longer exist.

- Epicurus

Mountains don't kill people, they just sit there.

- Ed Viesters

FAMILY AND OTHER SACRIFICES

I haven't collected a lot of quotes that fit the topic of "Family and Other Sacrifices," but it is such an important one for most pursuers of extreme sports that I couldn't ignore it. Whenever any of us leave on an adventure, we are leaving someone behind: a partner, a son, a parent, a friend. Someone stays behind to worry, to go to work and pay the bills, to manage the household, feed the cat, put out the garbage, and to hope and pray for our safe return.

Participating in extreme sports is ultimately a very selfish activity, and it is family members who end up making most of the sacrifices. I'm not sure what the divorce or break-up rates are for adventurers compared to the rest of the

177

masses, but it can't be good. Some understand these costs and continue to pursue their sport, some quit after a close call or the death of a colleague or threats of "either quit or I'm leaving." However, others are sadly oblivious to the sacrifices that others make while they pursue adventure. Some of our co-conspirators die and never come home.

I don't have any advice on this topic. I'm not sure what the ultimate right and wrong choices are when it comes to weighing the benefits of participating in extreme sports against the costs and sacrifices of the people we leave behind. I do know that there have been plenty of times that my son and my wife have given up a lot and felt abandoned and dumped on and fearful, while I've been off gallivanting around the world. I know that in these times I am being selfish and irresponsible, and I have to live with that.

If I fall off a mountain, to me it does not mean a thing. I come off, maybe five more seconds, and then I am dead. It's my wife, it's my two boys that are left behind.

- Peter Habeler

When you die, it negates the whole game: you haven't just fucked yourself, you've hurt lots of other people—that's when it becomes irresponsible and tragic.

- Greg Child

"If I die, I will wait for you, do you understand? No matter how long. I will watch from beyond to make sure you live every year you have to its fullest, and then we'll have so much to talk about when I see you again. . . ."

- Excerpt from *Halfway to the Grave* by Jeaniene Frost

Loving ourselves is crucial. If we do not love ourselves, how can we love others?

- Unknown

We must agree on what matters: kissing in public places, bacon sandwiches, disagreement, cutting-edge fashion, literature, generosity, water, a more equitable distribution of the world's resources, movies, music, freedom of thought, beauty, love.

- Salmon Rushdie

The risk taking is so much a part of his nature . . . if he stopped going away on these trips, I'm not sure he'd be the man I want to live with.

- Sue Ibara, describing her husband,
climber Mark Jenkins

Expeditions tend to disrupt your personal life, your financial life, and your health. The more you go on expeditions, the more chance there is of repeating all those disruptions.

- Jack Tackle

It is a beautiful necessity of our nature to love something.

- Douglas Jerrold

*"I was waiting for the longest time," she said. "I thought you forgot."
"It is hard to forget," I said, "when there is such an empty space when you are gone."*

- Excerpt from *Story People*
by Brian Andreas

Just because someone doesn't love you the way you want them to, doesn't mean they don't love you with all they have.

- Unknown

Q: What's the difference between a large pizza and a mountain guide?
A: A pizza can feed a family of four.

- Unknown

How does one reconcile the inevitable tension between such selfish and risky mountain play and the realities of that other life with its bonds and responsibilities?

- Tom Hornbein

When someone you love dies, and you're not expecting it, you don't lose him all at once; you lose him in pieces over a long time—the way the mail stops coming, and his scent fades from the pillows and even from the clothes in his closet and drawers. Gradually, you accumulate the parts of him that are gone. Just when the day comes—when there's a particular missing part that overwhelms you with the feeling that he's gone, forever—there comes another day, and another specifically missing part.

- Excerpt from *A Prayer for Owen Meany* by John Irving

Our relationship was like a precious, fantastic, jewel. It glowed, and it still glows, carrying me along. I'm stronger now, better able to deal with things. And I live more intensely.

- Widow of alpinist Andy Fanshawe, killed in Scotland while on a training climb for K2

"You'll stay with me?"
"Until the very end," said James.

> \- Excerpt from *Harry Potter and the Deathly*
> *Hallows* by J.K. Rowling

It is a curious thing, the death of a loved one. We all know
that our time in this world is limited, and that eventually all
of us will end up underneath some sheet, never to wake up.
And yet it is always a surprise when it happens to someone
we know. It is like walking up the stairs to your bedroom in
the dark, and thinking there is one more stair than there is.
Your foot falls down, through the air, and there is a sickly
moment of dark surprise as you try to readjust the way you
thought of things.

> \- Excerpt from *Horseradish: Bitter Truths*
> *You Can't* Avoid by Lemony Snicket

COMING BACK DOWN
THE MOUNTAIN

Climbers and adventurers all know that at some point at the end of an adventure you have to return to the real world, the place that is inhabited by the rest of humanity. You can't stay on the mountain forever. You can't avoid work and traffic and politicians and voicemail messages and unmowed lawns and unpaid bills forever. At some point you have to come back down the mountain.

There are a few ways to look at this reality of having to come back down. Some wonder, why even go to the top if you know that you have to come back down? What's the point? Why not just stay home and skip the pain, and expense, and frost-nipped fingers? If you know people that live in this space of "why even bother going," then maybe some of the quotes in this section will help them understand.

Rock climber Jeff Jackson once said, "Nobody cares what you sent [climbed]." That's one thing that I have realized over the years of coming back time and again from big expeditions. Beyond asking a polite question or two, very few people care about where I was or what I was doing, and fewer yet can relate to why I went, or the experiences I had. I have learned to share my thoughts on the pages of my journals, and maybe in a couple of brief email sentences to one of my few adventurer friends. I have a good friend, Jeff Budd from Alaska, who I used to get together with once every month or two for lunch at Lane 7, a local diner in Sitka that had six booths and the best milkshakes and curly fries in Southeast Alaska. Jeff and I would eat our fries and talk about an adventure we'd just finished, or the upcoming ones that we were cooking up in our heads. Jeff isn't a climber, he's more of a long distance biker and hiker, but he is one of the very few people in my life who understands without an explanation, why I was planning whatever hair-brained adventure was coming up next. I have always respected Jeff's sense of adventure and willingness to dream big dreams. Jeff Budd is guy who lives in the realm of possibility, not in the world of what can't be done. He knows what it's like to have an epic adventure and knows how it feels to return to ordinary life where we can't expect anyone to understand.

For most adventurers, whether we complete our goal or not, our journey or risky activity doesn't end up being a life changing experience. Book sales and speaking engagements are for the Hillarys and the Boningtons and not for the rest of us. But what most adventurers do share is that when we come back from our adventure, we return with a new or renewed appreciation for life, for the people we love, and for normal everyday things like flushing toilets, hot showers, and reading the paper. We come back with summit eyes, eyes that have seen the world from above, from a perspective that most people never have, or ever will. We return with a fresh perspective, a more informed perspective. The awareness of this fresh perspective is echoed by the words of T.S. Eliot, "And the end of all our journeying will be to return to the beginning of our travel, and to see it for the first time."

When I come back from a big climb, things seem clearer to me, more in focus. I come back appreciating my wife and my son even more. I come back appreciating my breathing more and my heartbeat more. I don't take sunsets for granted. I don't delay in responding to texts or phone calls from my son. I value, more than ever, sharing a cup of coffee and reading the paper with my wife. The challenge is to maintain that sense of appreciation for all things, especially for simple things. We must learn to maintain those summit eyes.

You can not stay on the summit forever,
You have to come down again . . .
So why bother in the first place?
Just this: What is above knows what is below;
But what is below does not know what is above.
One climbs, one sees. One descends, one sees no longer,
but one has seen.
There is an art of conducting oneself in the lower regions,
by the memory of what one saw higher up.
When one can no longer see, one can at least still know.

- Rene Daumal

Immediately after you stand on the peak of a mountain you
step forward and begin to climb a higher mountain which is
down below.

- Kobun Chino

You've climbed the highest mountain in the world. What's
left? It's all downhill from there. You've got to set your
sights on something higher than Everest.

- Willi Unsoeld

I had climbed my mountain, but I must still live my life.

- Sherpa Tenzing Norgay

There are other Annapurnas in the lives of men.

- Maurice Herzog

*I remember thinking that after that experience nothing
would ever upset me again, that I would be a different
person, that I had been miraculously saved for some
purpose that I didn't understand. But it didn't take very
long before I was back in the real world, a real person, and
nothing much had changed.*

- Dr. Charles Houston, after losing his
partner Art Gilkey on K2 in 1953

*Without doubt, the most important things have never been
standing on a summit, or reaching a Pole. Unquestionably,
it has been the work we have done in cooperation with the
mountain people, establishing schools, medical clinics, and
hospitals. Those are the things I will always remember.*

- Sir Edmund Hillary

Getting to the top is optional, getting down is mandatory.

- Ed Viesturs

After ecstasy, the laundry.

- Jack Kornfield

When one can no longer see, one can at least still know.

- Rene Daumal

The return home can be a rude awakening for the climber. For weeks or months, he has had a singular focus and a simple, uncluttered life. He has been out fighting dragons, moving through landscapes of mythical proportions, dealing with fundamental issues of courage and survival. Suddenly, he is back in the slow river of domestic life, a never ending flow of chores, demands, and small, mundane concerns. . . .

- Maria Coffey

The only guarantee in this fleeting market day we call life is that no matter how carefully you plod along, you'll grow old and get sick, or a force will sneak up in the dark and snuff you like piss on a campfire. Nobody is going to remember your hardest boulder problem or that you sent your project. After a few years, nobody cares who got the gold medal or the gold for that matter. Nobody cares who sent what, when, where, why, how. The memories fade, then just disappear and all that remains is the impact that you had on other people. Think about that.

- Jeff Jackson

You must know who you belong to, and who to come back to. I can not live without the mountains, but it is also true that I can not live without my family. I am in the middle, wired to both.

- Tomaz Humar

After the game, the king and pawn go into the same box.

- Italian Proverb

I never look at the masses as my responsibility; I look at the individual. I can only love one person at a time—just one, one, one. So you begin. I began—I picked up one person. Maybe if I didn't pick up that one person, I wouldn't have picked up forty-two thousand. . . . The same thing goes for you, the same thing in your family, the same thing in your church, your community. Just begin—one, one, one.

- Mother Teresa

I think a lot about climbing still, but not during the daytime. I think about it mostly at night, and on special occasions. I think about climbing when I am fed up with life in general. When I wish I could go over to the rocks or the trees. I enjoy my dreams about climbing.

- Fritz Wiessner, after a stroke
at the age of 87

Some say that the best climbers are the ones that are alive.

- Eric De Camp

The way I saw it, my life had been reduced to a handful of seconds, and now I had millions. . . . The value I'd learned from Jonathan's death, and my own near-death, was that sense of each moment.

- Rick Ridgeway

SOMETIMES YOU JUST HAVE TO SHAKE YOUR HEAD

A lot of the quotes I have collected over the years just don't fit cleanly into any particular category. Some are so deep I don't understand them, and some are just pretty damn funny. For whatever reason, they've stayed with me. They've remained in my quote files because even though they may be silly, they make me think. So, what do the quotes in this final chapter have to do with "adventuring inward" and risk taking? There are a lot of climbers and surfers and even every day risk takers who take themselves, their sports, and their actions way too seriously. Risk taking is a serious venture to be sure. Whether it's making an important decision about a relationship, or a job, or taking the risk to be honest, or taking a leap into the unknown, all of these things contain a level of sober thinking. Or at least they should. But equal to the danger of not taking the time to assess the potential outcomes of our actions and decisions is the risk of taking ourselves too seriously, becoming too self-important, and believing that we are better than the person next to us, no matter who that person is.

The famous playwright Oscar Wilde, who spent two years in prison and endured hard labor for "gross indecency" after it was discovered that he was in a relationship with another man, well understood the seriousness of his decisions, yet he also understood the importance of taking life too seriously. He has been quoted as saying that "Life is much too important a thing to ever talk seriously about it."

Adventure Inward: A Risk Taker's Book of Quotes focuses a lot on the serious topics of death, loss, family, transition, and making life choices and facing the consequences. But to stay sane, to remain human, we all have to maintain a sense of humor, and put our life and our struggles in a perspective that doesn't allow us to take ourselves too seriously. Here are a few quotes that make me chuckle, and others that really make me think. You may need to spend a few minutes with some of these quotes. Take your time.

Q. *"Yogi, what time is it?"*
A. *"You mean now?"*

- Yogi Bear

"Why do you keep robbing banks John?"
"Because that's where the money is."

- John Dillinger

Pissing is something that no one else can do for you. Only you can piss for yourself . . . [And] you must realize that to say, "Nobody else can piss for you," is to make an utterly serious statement.

- Soko Morinaga

My neighbor knocked on my door at 2:30 am this morning. Can you believe that? 2:30 am! Luckily for him, I was still up playing my bagpipes.

- Unknown

Once, I was lost in the wilderness, and I was forced to eat a dog to survive! Later I realized I was just in my back yard, but boy, was my mom pissed!

- C. Rostan

When elephants fight, it is the grass that suffers.

- Kikuyu Proverb

My view of Jesus is sort of like Elvis—love the guy, but not too sure about their fan clubs.

- Stephanie Miller

Nuclear war is winnable.

- Ronald Reagan

Fleas, lice,
*   The horse pissing*
*   Near my pillow.*

- Bashó

Eternity is a terrible thought. I mean, where's it going to end?

- Tom Stoppard

It's not music, it's a disease.

- Mitch Miller

I'd let Depends sponsor me if it meant I could give Everest a go.

- Unknown Climber

The more you complain, the longer God lets you live.

- Unknown

It's all bullshit on Everest these days.

- Sir Edmund Hillary

Friends help you move. Real friends help you move bodies.

- Unknown

Praise Allah, but first tie your camel to a post.

- Sufi Saying

We should make things as simple as possible, but not simpler.

- Albert Einstein

You're asking the wrong questions. If you want to make the world a better place, tell funnier jokes.

- Woody Allen

A good friend will bail you out of jail. A true friend will be sitting next to you in jail saying, "Damn . . . we fucked up."

- *Unknown*

I have only a small flickering light to guide me in the darkness of a thick forest. Up comes a theologian and blows it out.

- Denis Diderot

You have to stay in shape. My grandmother started walking five miles a day when she was sixty. Now she's ninety-seven and we don't know where the hell she is.

- Ellen DeGeneres

I had a linguistics professor who said that it's man's ability to use language that makes him the dominant species on the planet. That may be, but I think there's one other thing that separates us from animals. We aren't afraid of vacuum cleaners.

- Jeff Stilson

You can play a shoestring if you're sincere.

- John Coltrane

In baiting a mousetrap with cheese, always leave room for the mouse.

- Saki

Look wise, say nothing, and grunt. Speech was given to conceal thought.

- Sir William Osler

Three wandering monks, Seppo, Ganto, and Kinzan, had lost their way while making pilgrimage through the mountains. Then they spotted a green vegetable leaf floating down a stream, which meant that someone was living up the mountain. But they decided that anyone careless enough to lose one vegetable leaf was not worth meeting. Just then they saw a man with a long-handled hook racing along the stream, looking for his leaf.

- Zen Story

It's not what you don't know that hurts you, it's what you know that just aint' so.

- Satchel Paige

It's not as bad as it sounds.

- *Mark Twain, when asked what he thought of Wagner's music*

It's not advisable to drink too much strong liquors while climbing in the Alps. If, however, you are going to fall over a cliff, it's advisable to be thoroughly intoxicated when you do so.

- Unknown English Alpinist

Not only can I not recall my experiences in my previous lives, sometimes I can't even remember what I did yesterday.

- Dalai Lama

Since everything is none other than exactly as it is, one may well just break out in laughter.

- Long Chen Pa

The entire universe is the single eye of a monk. Where will you go to defecate?

- Hsueh-Feng

Climbers have no sense of smell.

- Conrad Anker's mother Helga

God hated reality but realized it was still the only place to get a good steak.

- Woody Allen

Strange new trend at the office. People putting names on food in the company fridge. Today I had a tuna sandwich named Kevin.

- Internet eCard

The most unfair thing about life is the way it ends. I mean, life is tough. It takes up a lot of your time. What do you get at the end of it? A Death! What's that, a bonus? I think the life cycle is all backwards. You should die first, get it out of the way. Then you live in an old age home. You get kicked out when you're too young, you get a gold watch, you go to work. You work forty years until you're young enough to enjoy your retirement. You do drugs, alcohol, you party, you get ready for high school. You go to grade school, you become a kid, you play, you have no responsibilities, you become a little baby, you go back into the womb, you spend your last nine months floating . . . and you finish off as an orgasm.

-George Carlin

WORKS CITED[2]

Brown, H. Jackson, Jr. *Life's Little Instruction Book.*
Nashville, TN: Rutledge Hill Press. 1991. Book.

Chadwick, David. *Crooked Cucumber: The Life and Teachings of Shunryu Suzuki.* New York: Broadway Books. 1999. Book.

Chouinard, Yvon. *180 Degrees South: Conquerors of the Useless.* Magnolia Pictures. 2009. Documentary.

Eliot, T.S. *The Waste Land.* 1922. Poem.

Emerson, Ralph Waldo. The complete works of Ralph Waldo Emerson: Poems [Vol. 9]. Boston: Belknap Press. 2011. Book.

Gibran, Khalil, *The Prophet.* New York: Alfred A. Knopf. 1923. Book.

Ingersoll, Robert Green. *Superstition and Other Essays.* NewYork: Prometheus Books. 2004. Book.

Johnson, Spencer. *The Precious Present.* New York: Doubleday Publishers. 1984. Book

Keller, Helen. *The Story of My Life.* New York: Doubleday, 1903. Book.

Kerouac, Jack. *Big Sur.* New York: Farrar Straus & Giroux. 1962. Book.

Kornfield, Jack. *Buddha's Little Instruction Book.* New York: Bantam Books. 1994. Book.

Lewis, C.S. *Shadowlands.* 1985. Television Film

Mellor, Don. *Rock Climbing: A Trailside Guide.* New York: W.W. Norton and Company, 1997. Book.

Montague, Charles E. "In Hanging Garden Gully," *Blackwood's Magazine.* Vol. CCXI, No. MCCLXXVI. Feb. 1922. Magazine.

Nietzsch, Friedrich. *The Gay Science: With a Prelude in Rhymes and an Appendix of Songs.* New York: Random House. 1974. Book.

Pirsig, Robert. *Zen and the Art of Motorcycle Maintenance.* New York: William Morrow and Company. 1974. Book.

Waterman, Jonathan. *The Quotable Climber.* New York: Lyons Press. 1998. Book.

---

[2] *This is a partial list of citations for quotes found only in the chapter introductions.*

ABOUT THE AUTHOR

Author Jon Wunrow is a parent, husband, adventurer, grant writer, cabin builder, Tribal consultant, adolescent therapist, and Green Bay Packer fanatic who occasionally finds time to plan and enjoy extreme adventures all over the world. In addition to pursuing his current goal of climbing the highest peak in every country in North, Central, and South America with his Australian climbing partner, he has also hiked the 2,650-mile Pacific Crest Trail, completed a two-month canoe trip in Northern Canada, climbed Kilimanjaro with his son Seth, and has had adventures in dozens of countries around the world. Some of his country high points include Denali (Alaska), Sajama (Bolivia), Aconcagua (Argentina), Orizaba (Mexico), and Julianna Top (Suriname). After living and raising his son in Sitka, Alaska for sixteen years, the author now resides in Bloomington, Indiana with his amazing and supportive wife, Leslie. Jon Wunrow is also the author of *High Points: A Climber's Guide to Central America (2012)*. Check out the author's website at *www.jonathanwunrow.com*

Made in the USA
Charleston, SC
28 May 2014